ENGAGING THE CONCERT AUDIENCE

A MUSICIAN'S GUIDE
TO INTERACTIVE PERFORMANCE

To access PDFs visit:
www.halleonard.com/mylibrary

8695-8721-3866-1867

DAVID WALLACE

For Eric Booth, who engages the world…

Berklee Press

Editor in Chief: Jonathan Feist
Senior Vice President of Online Learning and Continuing Education/CEO of Berklee Online: Debbie Cavalier
Vice President of Enrollment Marketing and Management: Mike King
Vice President of Online Education: Carin Nuernberg
Editorial Assistants: Emily Jones, Eloise Kelsey, Megan Richardson
Cover Design: Ranya Karafilly

ISBN: 978-0-87639-191-4

Study music online at
online.berklee.edu

DISTRIBUTED BY

HAL•LEONARD®
7777 W. BLUEMOUND RD. P.O. BOX 13819
MILWAUKEE, WISCONSIN 53213

1140 Boylston Street
Boston, MA 02215-3693 USA
(617) 747-2146

Visit Berklee Press Online at
www.berkleepress.com

Visit Hal Leonard Online
www.halleonard.com

Berklee Press, a publishing activity of Berklee College of Music, is a not-for-profit educational publisher.
Available proceeds from the sales of our products are contributed to the scholarship funds of the college.

Copyright © 2018 Berklee Press
All Rights Reserved

No part of this publication may be reproduced in any form or by
any means without the prior written permission of the Publisher.

CONTENTS

Acknowledgments.. v
Prelude: A Musical Quandary viii
PART I. The Art of Interactive Performance.......................... 1
    Chapter 1. What IS an Interactive Performance?.................... 3
    Chapter 2. Principles for Audience Engagement..................... 7
        Principle 1: Give the audience an entry point..................... 7
        Principle 2: Go beyond information,
                and engage through experience..................... 12
        Principle 3: Tap your audience's competence..................... 14
        Principle 4: Engage multiple intelligences........................ 16
        Principle 5: Reflect... 19
        Principle 6: Project your personality............................. 21
    Chapter 3. Designing Your Interactive Concert..................... 23
        Brainstorming the Theme and Repertoire....................... 23
        Designing Activities 26
        Scripting and Rehearsing the Concert 29
        Post-Performance Assessment................................... 30
    Chapter 4. Engage! Archetypes for Audience Interaction............ 31
        How Entry Points Work.. 31
        Interactive Archetypes and Strategies........................... 34
PART II. Deeper and Better Engagement 51
    Chapter 5. Developing an Engaging Stage Presence................. 53
        Speaking 57
        Movement and Stage Presence................................. 58
    Chapter 6. Avoiding Ten Common Pitfalls 63
        Pitfall 1: Too Many Words... 63
        Pitfall 2: Demonstration in Lieu of Discovery 64
        Pitfall 3: Under-Rehearsed Lines 66
        Pitfall 4: Under-Rehearsed Music................................ 67
        Pitfall 5: A Non-Musical Focus 69
        Pitfall 6: Irrelevant Activities 71
        Pitfall 7: Lack of Variety 73
        Pitfall 8: Failing to Be Audience Appropriate.................... 74
        Pitfall 9: Problematic Piece Lengths 75
        Pitfall 10: Disengaged Performers 76
    Chapter 7. Deeper Audience Engagement........................... 77
        Preconcert Workshops, Talks, and Events 78
        Concert Series 81
        Short-Term Residency 82
        Long-Term Partnerships and Residencies 83
        Following Up: Engaging Virtually................................ 85

PART III. Reaching Out in the Real World ... 87

Chapter 8. Engagement Everywhere: Performing in Schools, Hospitals, Prisons, Comedy Clubs, and More ... 89
- Schools ... 91
- Hospitals ... 92
- Psychiatric Facilities ... 94
- Correctional Facilities ... 96
- Houses of Worship and Religious Communities ... 100
- Comedy Clubs ... 102
- Bars, Cafés, Coffee Houses, and Nightclubs ... 104
- Busking ... 105

Chapter 9. Audience Engagement and Cultural Ambassadorship ... 109
- Overcoming Language Barriers ... 112
- Being a Musical Ambassador ... 114

Chapter 10. Straightforward Answers to Common Questions ... 119

Chapter 11. Engagement Is a Mindset ... 135

PART IV. Concert Transcriptions ... 139
- Application ... 139

Chapter 12. Improvisational Journey ... 141

What's So Great About Mozart? ... Online

The Secrets of Chamber Music ... Online

Myths and Legends ... Online

From Discord, Find Harmony: A Musical Exploration of Conflict and Resolution ... Online

Tchaikovsky's *Symphony No. 4* ... Online

Sound World ... Online

Rags, Riffs, and Reels ... Online

Appendix A. Interactive Concert Checklist ... 155

Appendix B. Annotated Bibliography ... 157

About the Author ... 160

Index ... 161

ACKNOWLEDGMENTS

I owe a tremendous debt of gratitude to:

- **Jonathan Feist,** for broadening and sharpening my focus, fully supporting this endeavor, editing skillfully
- **my loving family:** my sister Sheryl for providing the West-Texas writer's retreat that made this book a reality; my mother Marilyn for giving me a love of language; my father Charlie for introducing me to the joy of music
- **Robert Sherman,** whose vision and generous award made this book possible
- **the mentors and teachers who have shaped my philosophy and approach, especially:** Edward Bilous, Eric Booth, and Thomas Cabaniss of the Juilliard School; Polly Kahn of the League of American Orchestras; Jon Deak and Theodore Wiprud of the New York Philharmonic; and Hilary Easton, Jean Taylor, Maxine Greene, and Cathryn Williams of Lincoln Center Education
- **the wonderful people at The McGraw-Hill Companies who generously supported the first incarnation of this book:** Chris Freitag, Louis Haber, Jenny Katsoros, and Ed Stanford
- **the League of American Orchestras for encouraging this project from its inception**
- **the extraordinary administration, faculty, and students, of Berklee College of Music and the Boston Conservatory at Berklee**

ACKNOWLEDGMENTS

- **the concert presenters, educators, and benefactors who have embraced my ideas or encouraged my endeavors, especially:** Lester and Dinny Morse; Kay Churchill and Chris Silva of the Bardavon 1869 Opera House and the Hudson Valley Philharmonic; Marya Martin and Ken Davidson of the Bridgehampton Chamber Music Festival; Mark Wood and Laura Kaye of the MWROC Festival; Ann Gregg, Sarah Johnson, Deanna Keanett, Amy Rhodes, Aaron Siegel, and Rachel Sokolow of Carnegie Hall's Weill Music Institute; Laurie Carter, Teresa McKinney, Aaron Flagg, and Joseph Polisi of the Juilliard School; Alison Scott-Williams of the New Jersey Performing Arts Center; Rebecca Charnow of the Manhattan School of Music; Wayman Chin, Myran Parker-Brass, and Karen Zorn of Longy School of Music; Karen Demsey of William Paterson University; Ellen Highstein of the Tanglewood Music Center; Kazumichi Sunada, Michiko Oshima, and Sandie Nachigami of Japan's Life with Music Project; Matthew Loden and Bridget Anderson of Young Audiences of Houston; Richard Bell of Young Audiences, Inc.; Barb Day, Nancy Koepke, and Scott Seeburger of the Saginaw Community Enrichment Commission; Conductors William Prinzing Briggs, Marietta Cheng, Paul Gambill, Delta David Gier, Alan Gilbert, Alexander Mickelthwate, and Michael Tilson Thomas; Deborah Borda, Shino Fukui, Kristen Houkom, Toya Lillard, Zarin Mehta, Debora Kang, and Megan Lemley of the New York Philharmonic; Ed Barguiarena, Debbie Devine, Jessica Balboni, Rada Jovicic, Karl Montevirgen, Gretchen Nielsen, and Carolyn Palmer of the Los Angeles Philharmonic; Jessica Schmidt of the Boston Symphony Orchestra; James Hall of the Chicago Civic Orchestra; Robert Smith of the New World Symphony; Pace Sturdivant of the National Arts Centre Orchestra of Canada; Catherine Beeson of the Colorado Symphony; Penny Brill and Suzanne Perrino of the Pittsburgh Symphony Orchestra; Janet Bookspan, Donna East, Eric Ewazen, Eugene Friesen, Rev. James M. Hodsden, and Karen Ritscher

ACKNOWLEDGMENTS

- **the incredible teaching artists who have shaped and participated in this approach, especially:** Daniel Levy and Dana Scofidio, of the Doc Wallace Trio; April Clayton and Kristi Shade of Hat Trick; Angella Ahn, David Anzuela, Andrew Appel, Brad Balliett, Doug Balliett, Stacy Beam, John Bertles, Bridgid Bibbens, Chuck Bontrager, Lynn Brown, Bruce Brubaker, Claire Bryant, Kenji Bunch, Nicole Cherry, Linda Chesis, Julietta Curenton, David Cutler, Joe Deninzon, Keats Dieffenbach, Imani Douglass, Rushad Eggleston, Anna Elashvili, Gary Goldstein, Chelsey Green, Stephanie Griffin, Sean Grissom, William Harvey, Melissa Howe, Jerry James, Jerome Jennings, Russell G. Jones, Robert Kapilow, Barbara LaFitte, Zadie Lawler, Alicia Lee, Jessica Meyer, Michael Mizrahi, Beata Moon, Mark O'Connor, Carina Piaggio, Rachel Barton Pine, Evan Premo, Sarah Robinson, Daniel Bernard Roumain, Elizabeth Schwartz, Miranda Sielaff, Tracy Silverman, Uli Speth, Yale Strom, Mazz Swift, Saeunn Thorsteinsdottir, John Toth, Matt Vanacoro, Val Vigoda, Haydn Vitera, and Eli Yamin.

- **the musicians of the incomparable Teaching Artist Ensemble of the New York Philharmonic:** Amy Sue Barston, Meena Bhasin, Richard Carrick, Janey Choi, Jennifer Choi, Stanichka Dimitrova, Stephen Dunn, Kelly Dylla, Daniel Felsenfeld, Arnold Greenwich, Ani Gregorian Resnick, Chris Gross, Judith Hill Bose, Justin Hines, Sarah Skutel Holden, Jihea Hong-Park, Wendy Law, Andrea Lee, Colin McGrath, Jenny Ney, Emily Ondracek-Peterson, Elizabeth Janzen, Bridget Kibbey, Katie Kresek, Nora Kroll-Rosenbaum, Richard Mannoia, Paul Murphy, Paola Prestini, Andrew Roitstein, Rachel Shapiro, Misty Tolle, Laura Vincent, Erin Wight, Tanya Witek, and Airi Yoshioka

- **Chamber Music America, Young Audiences, Inc., and the numerous orchestras and who have given me a platform for sharing my ideas**

- **the countless friends, colleagues, musicians, and teachers** who believe and continue to contribute to this adventure.

PRELUDE

A Musical Quandary

During the winter of 1997, I wrestled with a musical quandary. I had just accepted a wonderful twenty-concert visiting-artist's residency in Saginaw, Michigan, but I wasn't sure how to make it work with my repertoire. After all, not every audience immediately appreciates highly polyphonic baroque works, Texas fiddling, free jazz, instrumental heavy metal, or atonal, contemporary pieces. Amidst the excitement of planning, my mind kept echoing the refrains of dubious concert-presenters and conductors:

"You can't play any contemporary music on our series; we have to consider our subscription base."

"Kids just don't like classical music."

"I wouldn't program any country music."

"I think you'd be better off if you presented a piece that told a story."

*"I really don't see how effective outreach can be done by **just one violist!**"*

As much as I hated these negative comments, I had to admit that each opinion was grounded in a stark reality. In order for my residency to succeed, I had to remove every barrier between me, my audience, and the music I loved. I needed a method for making the music come alive.

I spent the following months painstakingly figuring out how I could apply tried and true educational principles to a concert setting. The Juilliard School, the Lincoln Center Institute, and the New York Philharmonic had trained me in powerful methods of creative, experiential teaching that works wonders in long-term residencies, but could these tactics work in a concert?

By the end of the residency, I could answer with a definitive "Yes!" In the process, I had gathered several new proclamations to replace the former ones:

> "You play the best music I have ever heard."
>
> —Dustin, 4th grade

> "[The concert] was truly inspiring. So much that I have taken up private lessons again and am looking into attending Juilliard."
>
> —Amal, 10th grade

> "The song by J.S. Bach was cool."
>
> —Andie-ah, 5th grade

> "I have terminal cancer, and your concert just did me more good than all my chemotherapy treatments combined!"
>
> —A seventy-year-old Episcopal priest

I had found a powerful way to share my music and engage the audiences I so fervently wanted to reach. I am writing this book so that you and other musicians can do the same.

This book presents a method for opening and heightening your audiences' perceptions so that they are just as passionate about your music as you are. Most importantly, this method is grounded in music itself, not marketing shenanigans or extra-musical gimmicks. Various artists and ensembles have tested, refined, and contributed to this approach as it has continued to develop for more than twenty years. The ideas presented in this book represent contemporary practice, not just theory.

> ***"If you are a serious musician who wants to give your audience a deeper experience of music, this book is for you."***

Although many of my examples come from my work with classical musicians, this method has worked for performers of jazz, rock, bluegrass, hip-hop, Latin, folk, and other musical styles. If you are a serious musician who wants to give your audience a deeper experience of music, this book is for you. Let's go out and open some ears!

David Wallace
Chair, String Department, Berklee College of Music

PART I
The Art of Interactive Performance

CHAPTER 1

What IS an Interactive Performance?

What's an interactive performance?
  "A concert where the performers talk."
Really? What do they talk about?
  "They might say something about the music they're about to play, or the person who wrote it."
Oh. Does the audience get to do anything?
  "Sure. They can always ask whatever they like at the end of the show."

Hold it! Hold everything.

Unless I'm mistaken, the word "interact" implies that some sort of exchange is taking place. One person does something, which elicits a response, which results in a new situation, which generates another response, and the cycle continues. Cause and effect. Input-output. Give and take.

Interactive museum exhibits offer hands-on activity stations where visitors learn by participating. Interactive video games continually allow players to shape the direction and outcome of the game. Interactive comedians invite audience members onstage and improvise skits with them.

In an increasingly interactive world, why do so many musicians still think that an interactive performance is a concert where the performers talk while their silent, dutiful audience listens? If we publicize a performance as interactive, we must *interact*. Otherwise, let's call our event a lecture-demonstration and stop kidding ourselves.

So what is an interactive performance? For the purposes of this book, let's assume the following definition: An interactive performance is an event where the performers help audience members to perform, create, and reflect in ways that heighten their musical perceptions.

> *"An interactive performance is an event where the performers help audience members to perform, create, and reflect in ways that heighten their musical perceptions."*

We can accomplish this objective through countless means. To illustrate a few possibilities, here are four successful musical interactions from actual concerts:

- A conductor at the Tanglewood Music Festival teaches 2,000 audience members to perform along with the bass drum part to Aaron Copland's *Fanfare for the Common Man*.

- At a club, the leader of a jazz combo asks her audience to fill a hat with popular tune titles, which will be drawn by band members and quoted in their solos during the subsequent performance of "Sweet Georgia Brown." The drummer promises a free CD to anyone whose selected quote isn't used!

- To sensitize a high-school audience to the musical form and structure of twelve-bar blues, a singer gets his high-school audience to compose and sing two verses of an original blues song.

- To introduce the unconventional musical language of George Crumb's *Black Angels*, an electric string quartet helps the audience to create a piece that uses strange sounds and extended string techniques to evoke "images from the dark land." After the performance, the audience compares its compositional decisions to Crumb's.

Now we're interacting! Do you see the difference? In each of these instances, the performers personally involve their audiences in ways that heighten their musical experiences. The performers are not merely sharing information or teaching listeners about the music, nor are they doing flashy, entertaining things that fail to tap the audience's musical intelligence. Rather, they are enabling the audience to enter the specific world of each piece.

The conductor simply could have prefaced his performance of *Fanfare for the Common Man* with a brief biography of Aaron Copland or a discussion of the work's history. But as an audience member, would receiving that information match the thrill of performing one of Copland's masterpieces with the Tanglewood Festival Orchestra?

The jazz musician could have explained how soloists often sneak a fragment of a popular song into their improvisations. But would listeners feel the same excitement and payoff as when the band dared to let them have direct input into the solos?

Of course, genuine interaction entails a certain degree of risk. It might feel safer and easier just to talk. However, once you take the plunge and truly engage your audiences, you quickly discover that the payoffs far surpass any risks.

When you enable an audience to listen with a focused mind, a full heart, and active ears, there's a palpable electricity in the room. Nobody's daydreaming about what he's going to do after the concert. No one's critically comparing your interpretation to one she heard last fall. Everyone is focused on the music and the moment. Often, the audience will offer insights that may not have occurred to you, and your own perceptions of the music will deepen.

Heightened musical perception is the interactive performer's *raison d'être*. Such a performer learns to engage, educate, and entertain an audience, regardless of its demographic or level of musical expertise.

Interaction is more than a nice, extra touch for adding variety to our events; it is a vital component to the survival of live concert music. We must design events that meet a growing demand for hands-on, audience-centered experiences. We need performances that draw new listeners into deeper levels of musical comprehension and satisfaction. We need musicians who can actively engage every listener in the house.

> *"Interaction is more than a nice, extra touch for adding variety to our events; it is a vital component to the survival of live concert music."*

Interactive performance meets these critical needs. And unlike many audience-engagement strategies, interactive performance is artistically grounded and fun. All it requires is the intelligent application of a few principles, strategies, and skills. Let's learn them!

FIG. 1.1. David Wallace. The author performs "Bonaparte's Retreat" for a New York Philharmonic School Day Concert. Photo credit: Michael DiVito.

CHAPTER 2

Principles for Audience Engagement

Engaging interactive performances are grounded in six general principles:

1. Give the audience an entry point.
2. Go beyond information and engage through experience.
3. Tap your audience's competence.
4. Engage multiple intelligences.
5. Reflect.
6. Project your personality.

Grounding your concerts in these principles will guarantee that your listeners stay connected to the music.

PRINCIPLE 1: Give the audience an entry point.

Every piece of music contains elements that are central to its meaning, structure, and perception. When you sensitize listeners to one specific element, it becomes an entry point for listening actively and successfully.

You might think of an entry point as a compass for navigating the complexities of a musical work. Or a key you give listeners to unlock a particular piece.

Because every musical work can be understood and perceived in a variety of ways, any given work has several potential entry points. For example, the first movement of Beethoven's *Symphony No. 5* offers a variety of entry points: extreme dynamics, thematic contrast, suspense, orchestration, triumph, repetition, struggle, motives, thematic development, Beethoven's struggle with fate, and so on.

The success of Hank Williams's ballad "Your Cheatin' Heart" stems from many combined elements that could serve as entry points: honky-tonk vocal style, the steel guitar and fiddle's call-and-response, the use of melodic contour to tell a story, and the lyrics' universal message of love, betrayal, and loss.

An effective presentation conveys how a particular entry point functions in the work. It is better to explore one specific entry point in depth than to offer a smorgasbord of entry points in hopes that listeners will latch onto one of them. Think about which aspect would most successfully hook your listeners. Choose an entry point that will focus them for the duration of the work.

> **"It is better to explore one specific entry point in depth than to offer a smorgasbord of entry points in hopes that listeners will latch onto one of them."**

A conductor presenting the Beethoven movement to young children might lead an activity where they repeatedly whisper, speak, or shout the opening theme in an exploration of how extreme dynamics generate suspense and excitement. For an audience of high-school band and orchestra students, a musician from the orchestra might shed some light on Beethoven's use of sonata form by helping the audience to compose and develop two contrasting themes. Another conductor might awaken her subscription audience to the way Beethoven develops themes through orchestration by singing the opening theme, then asking the audience to choose instruments for performing it in series. In each of these scenarios, listeners have been introduced to a specific entry point to the symphony, and their attention has been focused via a direct experience.

A singer could open up "Your Cheatin' Heart" by leading the audience in some vocal explorations that incorporate yodeling, moving between head and chest voice, and finding ways to convey heartache and pain with the voice. A band member could join in and help volunteers to improvise call-and-response piano phrases in relation to the vocal explorations. When the band finally plays the song (and subsequent songs), the audience is attuned to vocal nuance and band interaction.

When we present entry points in this open, exploratory manner, listeners make their own discoveries as they listen. They go beyond merely identifying information we have given or demonstrated for them. This interactive application of an entry point is what jumpstarts the meaning-making process. *An entry point does not serve as well if we just talk about it.*

Jerry James, a visual artist and the Center for Arts Education's Director of Teaching and Learning, often relates arts appreciation approaches to the ways people can experience an ice cream cone. If all we do is talk about an entry point, or our own interpretations of a work, it's like holding up an ice cream cone and describing what eating it is like.

When we give the audience a hands-on exploration of an entry point, we hand them an ice cream cone and let them taste it for themselves. In the above Beethoven and Hank Williams examples, the performers have transcended passive explanation by offering listeners a first-hand "taste" of the musical ingredients.

Without a hands-on experience of an entry point, uninitiated listeners may find themselves baffled, intimidated, or bored by complex or unfamiliar music. The first time I heard Jimi Hendrix's guitar, the vocals of Janis Joplin and Robert Plant, and the chamber music of Béla Bartók, I was overwhelmed by the intensity and the dissonance.

Oh, I vividly remember my first encounter with Bartók string quartets as a sixteen-year-old audience member. Up until that point in my life, I had only heard or studied string quartets by Haydn, Mozart, Beethoven, Mendelssohn, Schubert, and Tchaikovsky.

Largely unacquainted with twentieth-century musical language, I found Bartók's music dissonant, strident, raucous, and generally lacking melody and form. I concluded that Bartók was a horrible composer, and I became determined to avoid his music at all costs.

What went wrong that evening? In hindsight, I can't blame the performance; a famous quartet was clearly playing its heart out. Bartók's quartets are widely regarded as masterpieces, so this wasn't a case of poor repertoire.

Naive as I may have been about twentieth-century music, I was not an "ignorant, uncultured person who just needed more concert experience." Rather, I was a life-long music lover and a serious violinist. Nevertheless, as hard as I tried, I found no way to listen successfully to the music. No matter how much the quartet or anyone else was enjoying the concert, I felt left out.

I needed an entry point. I needed someone to take me inside Bartók's musical mind and language so that I could understand the unfamiliar harmonies, timbres, and intervals.

Today, Bartók's music makes perfect sense to me because I have had subsequent experience studying and performing it. However, my comfort with Bartók's music does not guarantee that my own audiences can successfully hear it. They will only share my enjoyment if they have an entry point.

By the same token, you must find ways to connect listeners to the music you love. If you love hip-hop, you need to build a bridge to enlighten people who resist it. Whether your heart's desire is to make a living playing bebop, extreme metal, old-time fiddling, classical music, or classic funk, be prepared to expand your audience and bring others into your world.

CONSIDER THIS: POTENTIAL ENTRY POINTS

Below are some categories of entry points to consider as you design your presentations. These lists are far from comprehensive. Expand them by adding your own entry points as you discover them.

Musical Elements

- Melody (melodic contour, specific themes and motives, melody vs. accompaniment, scales, modes, embellishment and ornamentation. . .)
- Harmony (parts playing in harmony, major vs. minor, consonance vs. dissonance, tone clusters, diminished chords. . .)
- Counterpoint (contrapuntal forms, imitation, canon, fugue, basso continuo)
- Rhythm (beat, meter, rests, tempo, cross rhythms, subdivision, dotted rhythms, triplets, syncopation, polyrhythms, groove, dance beats, ostinato, tempo changes. . .)
- Form (binary, ABA, rondo, sonata form, 12-bar blues, 32-bar song structure, theme and variations. . .)
- Dynamics
- Articulation (legato, staccato, accents. . .)
- Timbre (sound of instruments, special effects, mutes, multiphonics, harmonics, pizzicato, orchestration, vocal range, electronic effects. . .)
- Genre and style

Common Metaphors Used to Express Musical Ideas

- Layers (foreground and background, rhythmic layers, instrumental layers)
- Conversation (dialogue, argument, interruption, antecedent-consequent phrase structure)
- Tension and release
- Contrast (instruments, dynamics, articulation, themes. . .)
- Mood (gloomy, peaceful, manic, anxious. . .)
- Emotion (sorrow, joy, anger, disappointment, surprise, love, hate. . .)
- Energy (rhythmic, dynamic, tempo. . .)
- Patterns (melodic, rhythmic, harmonic, formal)
- Texture
- Surprise
- Echoes
- Transformation

Additional Aspects Related to Specific Works:

- Narrative or programmatic content (stories, sounds and depictions of nature, poems. . .)
- Characters (especially in operatic works, musicals, or songs)
- Word-painting
- Style (genre, dance forms, folk influences, national characteristics)
- Biographical or historical context

PRINCIPLE 2: Go beyond information, and engage through experience.

Going back to Jerry's ice-cream cone metaphor, your goal is to give your audience a hands-on experience of your chosen entry point. This approach differs radically from traditional music appreciation methods, which tend to rely heavily on verbal information.

Information is not a bad thing. It can introduce contexts and clarify concepts. Some listeners, especially adults, are quite hungry for information, and we do well to provide it. However, *unless information is grounded in an actual experience, it seldom helps a listener's ears.*

Consider my Bartók predicament. Would knowing Béla Bartók's birth and death dates help me to hear counterpoint in his quartets? Would a dictionary definition of *counterpoint* really offer any substantial assistance? Would facts about Bartók's life enable my ears to digest chords and timbres that sounded painfully caustic?

If I had been given such information, I may have listened with a little more contextual understanding. However, contextual knowledge would not necessarily have affected my musical perception. Informed audience members may feel successful on an intellectual level, but without an experience, their ears remain fundamentally unaltered.

> **CONSIDER THIS: APPRECIATING BARTÓK**
> What kinds of experiences might have opened my sixteen-year-old ears to the greatness of Bartók's music?
> - After demonstrating a few of Bartók's stringed instrument "special effects," from the *String Quartet No. 4*, the ensemble could collaborate with the audience to create a one-minute piece that uses these unconventional sounds. Allowing me to explore Bartók's timbres creatively would allow me to perceive them more deeply.
> - To introduce Bartók's melodic language, the quartet could teach the audience to sing one of the Hungarian folk songs he collected—one that is melodically and rhythmically related to a movement that follows. Having sung in Bartók's melodic language, I could process his melodies more easily.
> - The ensemble could have led the audience in a clapping activity that uses Bartók's rhythmic motives to introduce the concepts of imitation and counterpoint.
> - Before hearing the *Quartet No. 6*, the audience could be led to reflect on their own experiences of alienation or loss. Entering Bartók's emotional mindset would prepare them to be moved more deeply than if they were merely told the biographical context of the work.

Admittedly, this approach is a departure from more conventional ways of doing things, but you can find precedent for it in the work of Leonard Bernstein, Pete Seeger, and other music educators of the twentieth century. Chapter 4 will provide plenty of ideas for creating and executing these kinds of activities.

When you design an audience interaction, give experience priority over information. Information shared after or during an experience is far more likely to be received and remembered.

FIG. 2.1. Michael Tilson Thomas conducts the audience at a San Francisco Symphony Gala. Photo by Kristen Loken.

PRINCIPLE 3: Tap your audience's competence.

You perform for an audience of experts. Your listeners may *think* they're musically unskilled, or unknowledgeable about your particular kind of music, but you can prove them wrong by taking advantage of capabilities and knowledge they already possess. Audience members enter the performance space with many skills and abilities—including musical ones—which we can exploit in ways that are relevant to the music that follows.

When we get an audience to sing a theme, clap a rhythmic accompaniment, or make creative and interpretive decisions about music, we put the listeners in our shoes. They become performers and creators. They experience the joys and challenges of making music and gain confidence in their abilities to make musical connections.

CONSIDER THIS: WHAT AN AUDIENCE CAN DO

With the help of many musicians, I have been compiling a list of "Things Audience Members Can Do." Here are categorized highlights from the list, which will give you an idea of the skills you can tap through your activities. Again, you should expand this list as you develop and discover new approaches to tapping audiences' competence.

Things Audience Members Can Do:

Ways Audiences Can Produce Sounds:
- Sing, hum, whistle...
- Make vocal sounds expressing moods, objects, animals
- Play instruments
- Make use of body percussion/snap, clap, stamp...
- Make sounds of different timbres and dynamics

Other Musical Capacities:
- Keep a steady beat
- Echo call-and-response patterns
- Harmonize
- Conduct (tempo, meter, dynamics, articulation, cue, and cutoff...)
- Respond to conducting signals
- Coach musicians on how to play
- Make aesthetic choices about how to interpret music
- Compose original melodies, rhythms, and themes
- Make compositional choices
- Determine the repertoire or the program order
- Improvise on percussion instruments or with the voice
- Learn and perform melodies and rhythms either independently or perform these patterns as accompaniments
- Perform with the musicians
- Perform as a member of a section

Ways Audiences Can Respond to Music:
- Stand up and move (dance, jog, or march in place)
- Sway from side to side
- Rock back and forth
- Make hand signals and hand motions
- Express themselves through gestures/point
- Listen or watch for something specific
- Analyze, reflect, or discuss something they have heard
- Express observations and interpretations of the music
- Light lighters or wave cell phones
- Play "air guitar" and other instruments

> **Additional Capacities:**
> - Solve puzzles or riddles
> - Play games
> - Vote
> - Volunteer
> - Help musicians demonstrate a concept
> - Move or dance
> - Act in skits
> - Make facial expressions
> - Work with a partner
> - Tell jokes
> - Work in a small group
> - Converse with a musician or host/have a discussion with a neighbor/ask and answer questions
> - Paint or draw shapes and pictures/draw a shape in the air
> - Recognize visual or aural patterns
> - Write
> - Think, visualize, and imagine
> - Recall memories and emotions
> - Use social media

Application

As an exercise, pick an entry point from the list of entry points (e.g., "ABA form"). Now, look at the "Things Audience Members Can Do" list, and design a few activities that would give the audience a hands-on experience of your chosen entry point. For example:

1. Physicalize ABA form through body motions (e.g., run in place/march in place/run in place).
2. Sing a familiar song in ABA form.
3. Have some volunteers create some ABA patterns by drawing geometric shapes.

Try this with a few entry points. How many different activities can you create?

PRINCIPLE 4: Engage multiple intelligences.

Although our listeners bring competences into the hall, their perceptual abilities and preferences can be quite diverse. Some people are kinesthetic learners who best learn by physically doing something. Others are highly verbal and prefer books and written instructions. Still others rely on strong visual and spatial skills to interpret the world around them.

When performing, we have a responsibility to connect with all of our listeners. If our presentation addresses only one perceptual style, we may fail to connect with many other audience members. One of the surest ways to connect with everyone in our audience is to target different modes of perception. Harvard Professor Howard Gardner's groundbreaking multiple intelligence theory provides an excellent guideline for addressing diverse perceptual styles.

In his book *Frames of Mind*, Gardner identified seven distinct "intelligences," which enable people to perceive and process the world. In theory, we all possess each of these capacities, to a greater or a lesser degree. For each intelligence, I provide a short explanation and an example of how you might engage it during a concert:

- **Visual/Spatial Intelligence** processes the images we see. Televised musical broadcasts use strategic camerawork to tap our visual/spatial intelligence. By zooming in on instruments at the moment that they perform themes or important accompaniments, the camera focuses our listening. Live concerts in many genres use similar video projections, but we can achieve a similar effect through careful use of lighting and staging. Pictures, projected images, animations, light shows, and film are just a few means of stimulating our visual/spatial intelligence.

- **Verbal/Linguistic Intelligence** encompasses our ability to acquire, process, and use language and words. As performers, we often converse and explain, but we should also consider creative ways of tapping our audience's verbal/linguistic intelligence. Commonly, performers teach song lyrics and chants (or help audience members to create them). Others encourage the audience to create metaphors and similes as a means of entering the poetic world of the songwriter.

- **Logical/Mathematical Intelligence** encompasses our aptitude for logic, numbers, and reasoning, both deductive and inductive. While this intelligence may initially seem less applicable to interactive performance, we can actually use it to exciting effect. Our audiences enjoy solving deductive puzzles, recognizing or composing musical patterns, performing complex rhythmic patterns, and so forth. This intelligence also helps listeners to understand musical form and structure.

- **Bodily/Kinesthetic Intelligence** involves physical coordination skills. Any activity that entails movement, dance, or physical action requires bodily/kinesthetic intelligence. Choreography or conducting activities can be particularly useful when they incorporate expressive movement and breathing.

- **Musical/Rhythmic Intelligence** encompasses musical creation, performance, and appreciation. Obviously, any kind of performing, composing, or listening activity requires musical intelligence. If we're doing our job right, we'll be engaging this intelligence every step of the way, even as we tap other modes of perception.

- **Interpersonal Intelligence** is our ability to understand, empathize, and communicate with others. In concerts, interpersonal intelligence is most commonly tapped through conversation, but it is also involved in empathetically grasping what the performer is expressing.

- **Intrapersonal Intelligence** is our capacity for introspection, self-knowledge, and self-awareness. This critical capacity helps us establish personal interpretations and connections to the music. It also enables us to develop a sense of how to listen successfully. Intrapersonal intelligence is tapped by activities that encourage reflection, personal interpretation, or an awareness of how we react to musical passages.

When designing a fully interactive concert, aim to address each intelligence at least once during the course of the event. When you address more than one intelligence when setting up a piece, you will more likely engage the entire audience.

Application

As an exercise, go back to the "Things Audience Members Can Do" list (page 15), and identify the intelligence(s) that correspond to each ability. (E.g., "Clap a rhythm" involves kinesthetic and musical intelligences; "Recognize visual or aural patterns" suggests visual/spatial intelligence and logical/mathematical intelligence.)

PRINCIPLE 5: Reflect.

While fast-paced presentation can be exciting and desirable, we need to make sure that every piece sinks in. Reflective moments deepen musical experiences and allow them to settle.

One of my favorite places to perform is a public library in Bethpage, Long Island, where there is a series called *Conversations with Music*. At these events, performers spend an hour performing and conversing with the audience, which consists of approximately a hundred retirees who have a passion for music. One of the most rewarding aspects of these events is their highly investigative nature.

After I perform selections, the audience has an opportunity to share its perceptions with one another and with me. We put the music under a collective microscope. With my instruments and voice, I can demonstrate passages that affirm or clarify people's observations and questions.

Often, all I need to do to stimulate the conversation is to ask three simple questions.[1] To elicit some initial perceptions, I ask, "So what struck you about this piece?" When someone offers an interpretation that begs further exploration (e.g., "It sounded to me like Paganini was trying to be a diva."), I ask, "What about the music makes you say that?" This non-threatening question leads observers to articulate the specific musical details behind their interpretations. Often, their comments address musical subtleties that I might not have considered myself. Finally, to elicit additional observations, I ask, "Did anyone hear anything else?"

Our individual perspectives are enriched by reflecting on our collective responses. By stopping to notice what we perceived, our listening experience becomes more deeply implanted in our memories.

---

1. These questions, learned through Lincoln Center Institute training, were adapted from Visual Thinking Strategies (VTS), a method developed by Visual Understanding in Education (VUE) for exploring works of visual art.

> *"Reflection can nudge the audience from the realm of passive entertainment into the deeper world of personal, aesthetic response."*

Reflection can nudge the audience from the realm of passive entertainment into the deeper world of personal, aesthetic response. Of course, not every performance situation is conducive to the intimate dialogue possible at Bethpage. However, any performance has ample opportunity to encourage the audience to think introspectively and interpretively.

Some performers prepare their audiences emotionally by asking questions that evoke memories related to the mood of a subsequent piece. Others ask intriguing aesthetic or compositional questions that cause the audience to listen from a composer's perspective (e.g., "If you wanted to write some dangerous-sounding music, how would you do that?").

A successful tactic I have seen applied to audiences of all ages and sizes is to pause for a brief moment to have everyone discuss a question with a partner. Ernest Schelling's New York Philharmonic Young People's Concerts from the 1920s–30s even gave children opportunities to write brief responses in a musical journal.

Reflection doesn't always need to involve dialogue or writing. Some musicians have asked audience members to share their musical reactions by striking poses, making facial expressions, or drawing pictures.

When you script a concert, be sure to plan reflective moments and activities. Whether used to prepare the audience to hear a piece or to reexamine it, the extra reflective steps can make the musical experience a lasting memory.

PRINCIPLE 6: Project your personality.

Teaching artists Eric Booth and Edward Bilous often share the adage, "80 percent of what you teach is who you are." For better or for worse, an audience's musical response is deeply affected by its perception of us. If we appear disengaged or dispassionate, the audience has no incentive to receive our performance. On the other hand, our passions and personalities can inspire listeners in ways that recordings and textbooks cannot.

> *"Our passions and personalities can inspire listeners in ways that recordings and textbooks cannot."*

Most performers with substantial followings and successful careers have earned them in part because they project their extraordinary personalities when they perform and speak. Top-grossing pop stars offer fans a variety of attractive images which range from the fun and vivacious party animal to the glamour girl or anti-hero. In each case, the personality of the performer heightens the audience's enthusiasm for the music.

In the classical world, Leonard Bernstein's charisma and enthusiasm led an entire generation to appreciate symphonic music. Violinist Itzhak Perlman's warmth and sense of humor charms any audience regardless of its experience with classical music.

As an interactive performer, your personality will naturally come into play in your concerts. This doesn't mean that you have to act, adopt an unnatural persona, or be as charismatic or controversial as the current chart-topping artist. It does mean that your programs should reflect your own musical interests and passions and that you should be willing to share them. Choose repertoire that excites you. Be willing to share relevant anecdotes or information about yourself. If you're comfortable with yourself and enthusiastic about what you're doing, your audience will be, too.

CHAPTER 3

Designing Your Interactive Concert

Designing an interactive performance takes considerable time and effort at first, but the more you do it, the easier the process becomes. For a variety of reasons, I encourage you to design concerts collaboratively rather than individually.

Working with like-minded colleagues usually facilitates and enriches the planning process, even for solo artists or musicians who prefer to work independently. When ensemble or band members contribute to programming, designing, and scripting, they tend to participate more actively during the actual performance. However, if some members of your group are anxious or reluctant to interact in performance, you may need to assume the leadership in planning and presenting.

Designing an interactive concert encompasses four basic processes, which often overlap: brainstorming the theme and repertoire, designing activities, scripting and rehearsing the concert, and assessing the performance. This sounds basic, and it is. Nevertheless, how you approach each stage can dramatically affect the quality of your final presentation.

BRAINSTORMING THE THEME AND REPERTOIRE

During the initial planning stages, your goal is to determine your concert's theme and musical content.

A good interactive concert theme fulfills four basic criteria:
1. The theme is intriguing, challenging, or entertaining for both the performers and the audience.
2. The theme invites musical exploration, not just demonstration.
3. The theme has an emotional or intellectual "bite."
4. The theme is musically strong and original.

Rather than elaborate on these qualifications in the abstract, let's examine a few successful themes, which met them quite well:

- **The Different Moods of the Blues:** Composer, singer, pianist, and bandleader Eli Yamin developed a show that presented a vast and diverse sampling of blues repertoire through history, but with a strong focus on how the blues can reflect human emotion and heal. The band tapped listeners' emotions, rhythmic abilities, and voices in order to unlock the groove, the message, and the musical and poetic form. On a surface level, the audience was hearing a great concert. On a deeper level, the audience was developing the emotional, cognitive, and analytical skills to emotionally connect—and become a living part of—a rich and complex tradition.

- **Orchestral Survivor!:** The Fort Wayne, Indiana Philharmonic has a hip "unplugged" series, which offers interactive performances for an adult audience. At the height of the *Survivor* television series' popularity, the orchestra designed a "Survivor" concert, complete with totem poles and flaming torches. The various sections of the orchestra competed against one another, completed challenges, and campaigned against the other sections while touting their own section's strengths. One by one, the audience voted sections of the orchestra off of the stage, until only one section remained to play the concert's finale. (Despite a percussionist's complaint that the violin tribe should be eliminated because they hog all the notes, the strings were the last section standing—by a margin of five votes.)

- **The Fisk Jubilee Singers, Uniting Voices:** The Perelman American Roots Program of Carnegie Hall's Weill Music Institute created a residency and concert featuring the renowned Fisk Jubilee Singers. Designed for an audience of New York City middle-school and high-school students, the preparatory workshops focused on a potent question: "How have African-American songs united people, expressed perspectives, and effected cultural and spiritual change?" Prior to the concert, students learned many spirituals, created vocal arrangements of them, wrote original songs expressing their own responses to social ills, and did a great amount of contextual research. A culminating experience, the concert allowed the audience to sing and perform as a direct means of witnessing and becoming a part of the living history of the Fisk Jubilee Singers.

- **Sound World:**[2] The Teaching Artist Ensemble of the New York Philharmonic created a concert featuring music of composers from five continents. The concert answers the question, "How do composers create the musical sounds of their cultures?" Highly participatory, the audience learns rhythms, melodies, and dance steps as they begin to analyze and internalize the sound world of each composer.

Each of these concert themes succeeds because it addresses musical issues that are compelling to performer and audience alike. When beginning your planning process, take the time to develop a theme with rich possibilities and interesting implications. A good, highly marketable theme strategically taps the natural curiosity and interests of the audience. It suggests a fun, humorous, or thought-provoking experience. A good theme also is attuned to the natural abilities and personality of your ensemble.

Intriguing themes often revolve around a question. When given the challenge of presenting a school concert about American music, a Manhattan School of Music brass quintet considered the following questions as potential organizing themes: *What makes music sound American? How did the development of American musical styles parallel American history? How does American classical music reflect contemporary American culture?* Each question suggests a rich and specific inquiry that can be explored with much more depth and variety than a generic "Here's some American music" presentation.

Once you have decided your theme, finalize your repertoire. Note the duration of each selection, and consider possible program orders. Do you want your set list to be surprising? Cyclical? Emotionally shaped? Logically structured? Without interaction, would the concert still feel musically satisfying?

---

2. The full transcript of this interview is available online. See the title page of this book for how to access it.

Usually, it is nice to begin with an attention-grabbing segment and to culminate with something that ties all of the elements of your presentation together. Your intervening selections and activities should offer a variety of tempos, styles, durations, or moods. Many musicians have reported that it is helpful to have a slightly longer or more substantial work as an "anchoring work" or "main course."

In general, a "two-thirds music and one-third interaction" formula is ideal for a fully interactive performance. In other words, if you are preparing a 45-minute program, you should aim to have about 30 minutes of music and 15 minutes devoted to preparatory activities, reflection, and questions.

DESIGNING ACTIVITIES

When you design activities, begin by investigating each of your selections in depth. Listen to a work several times, jotting down your impressions from each hearing. First, listen for pleasure, and note any initial impressions and reactions. Next, pretend to be the typical audience member who will attend your event, and do your best to listen through their ears. This step is particularly helpful when preparing presentations for children or non-musicians. Finally, listen with your analytical perspective as a trained musician—preferably while reading a score, if you have one. If you are planning a concert as a group, each member can assume one of these roles, and you can share your diverse observations after just one hearing.

Listening from multiple perspectives will help you to describe, analyze, and interpret each work fully. From your observations, it will be relatively easy to generate a list of potential entry points. After brainstorming entry points for all of the works, circle the entry points that best illuminate each work while supporting your concert's theme.

> **CONSIDER THIS: THE RIGHT ENTRY POINT**
> When searching for the right entry point, some helpful questions to ask are:
> - What makes this work great? What excites me about it?
> - What do I especially hope my audience notices?
> - Is there anything unusual, cool, or striking about the work?
> - Is there any musical element or metaphor that underpins the entire piece?
> - What entry points would make good aural or visual "hooks" for first-time listeners?
> - What difficulties would a first-time listener encounter in this work?
> - Is there anything programmatic or historical about the work that would help a listener?
> - What aspects of this piece are so strong and immediate that they need no activities to highlight them?

Once you have selected entry points for each work, design activities that will draw the audience into the work via those entry points. Make the activities as hands-on and experiential as possible. Strive for a variety of presentational formats, and address different perceptual styles.

Application

Useful questions for designing activities around an entry point:

In what ways does this concept manifest itself in my audience's everyday life?

How can this concept be experienced:

- by a physical activity?
- by a visual aid or a visual activity?
- by singing, making sounds, or playing musical instruments?
- by a dramatic sketch?
- through an analogy or anecdote?

How could the entire audience actively illustrate this concept? One volunteer? A group of volunteers?

Refer to your list of "Things Audience Members Can Do" (page 15) for additional interactive ideas.

When you choose your entry point, be sure that it really underpins the piece you are performing. Also, make sure that your activity conveys how the entry point functions in the musical work.

Sometimes, musicians lead brilliant activities that sensitize the audience to one spectacular moment, but for the rest of the piece, the listeners are left in the dark. Other times, musicians create generic activities that teach a concept well, but fail to illuminate the music because the activity has not been tailored to the specific work.

One fascinating example that demonstrates both shortcomings comes from a good friend who was conducting a youth orchestra's family concert entitled *Wake Up and Smell the Orchestra: A Concert of Morning Music*.

At the beginning of the concert, a few musicians (a violinist, a flutist, a tuba player, and a triangle player) were to step forward to audition for the distinction of "best musical alarm clock"—a very fun, inquiry-based activity. Much to the tuba player's disappointment, the dress-rehearsal audience ultimately voted that they would prefer to wake up to a triangle.

Next, the orchestra performed the opening of Richard Strauss's *Also sprach Zarathustra* (made famous by Stanley Kubrick's film, *2001: A Space Odyssey*). At the climax of the opening, the percussionist dutifully entered with Strauss's extended triangle roll.

The triangle roll was a cool moment. Most people commented that they had never consciously noticed it before, and they were grateful to have been led to discover it. The preparatory activity was fun and entertaining. The piece was a great concert-opener. Nevertheless, the conductor was dissatisfied with himself. He felt that in many regards, his presentation had missed the mark:

> "The more I listened to people's feedback, the more I realized I was leading them in the wrong direction. After all, is Richard Strauss's **Also sprach Zarathustra** really about a triangle roll? Is that what's so awe-inspiring about it? What about the brass fanfare? The pounding timpani solos? The deep pedal tones of

the bass instruments? Is the literary work that inspired Strauss, Friedrich Nietzsche's ***Also sprach Zarathustra***, a meditation on alarm clocks? No! It's about a deeper kind of awakening..."

To illumine Strauss's music more fully, the activity was adjusted so that the instrumentalists who auditioned would be those who play important themes in this introduction. Instead of inventing their own "alarm clock sounds," they would audition with Strauss's themes or a similar phrase. (In the case of the brass, the conductor composed and substituted a similar fanfare so that Strauss's instantly recognizable theme would remain a surprise at the performance.)

Instead of voting for which instrument sounded the most like an alarm clock, families in the audience were led to discuss, "If this instrument were an alarm clock, what kind of person or creature would wake up to it?" After sharing suggestions, the conductor complimented the audience on how "awake" their imaginations were. He then related how Strauss was using music to demonstrate Nietzsche's ideas about the awakening of the imagination and the human spirit. During the performance, listeners could notice how all the instruments and themes combined to create a monumental sense of awakening.

—And they still noticed the triangle roll.

SCRIPTING AND REHEARSING THE CONCERT

As the activities emerge, you may wish to change the program order. Some concert designers and artistic directors believe that it is best to end the concert with the most interactive, participatory part to avoid an anticlimax.

Once you have the overall structure finalized, write a script for your concert. The script can range from a succinct one-page outline to an elaborate script with prepared dialogue. If you take the former approach, be thorough and specific; if you take the latter, be sure to allow room for flexibility, spontaneity, and audience response. In most situations, it's best to prepare both a one-page outline and a formally written script. Whatever you do, avoid reading your script during the performance.

When creating your script, plan effective transitions from preparatory activity to performance and from each work to the next. Highlight relationships between the different pieces, and include reflective moments.

Once your script is essentially completed, begin rehearsing. Run the script a few times without the music. The activities and spoken parts of the concert should be given at least as much rehearsal time as the musical parts. Once you are comfortable performing the entire program, hold a dress rehearsal for an audience of your colleagues, your family, or anyone who is available and willing to participate. The dress rehearsal will highlight any rough places that need to be reworked, reworded, or refined. Audio and video recordings of the rehearsal can provide extremely helpful feedback.

POST-PERFORMANCE ASSESSMENT

After your performance, take time to assess it. Interview audience members about their experiences. What struck them about the performance? What were their favorite parts and pieces? Written questionnaires or online polls can provide extremely helpful feedback, as well as useful quotes for your press kit. If you have hired a videographer, he or she can interview the audience as they leave the performance.

As a group and with colleagues, watch a video recording of your concert. Make observations and comments. Are there any moments that particularly stand out? Which parts engaged the audience the most? Why? What could you do next time to make those successes even deeper or better? What feedback did you receive from the audience after the performance?

Note any adjustments you found yourself making during the performance. What did you learn? If something didn't work out as well as you had planned, determine the reasons. Did the audience need clearer instructions? Did an activity need one or two additional steps in order for it to work?

Find additional venues for performing this program, and start designing your next one!

CHAPTER 4

Engage! Archetypes for Audience Interaction

Now that you understand the underlying principles of interactive concerts, let's examine the fundamental types of audience interaction. Since every interaction is centered on an entry point, let's first consider how we can use entry points most effectively.

HOW ENTRY POINTS WORK

Entry points can help people to appreciate musical works in essentially three ways: on a purely musical level, on an intellectual/metaphorical level, or on a personal, emotional level.

For example, a pianist may decide that the driving force behind a Chopin prelude is the desire for harmonic resolution. Her chosen entry point is consonance and dissonance. A presentation that contrasts the instability of diminished chords with the stability of major and minor triads would address listeners on a purely musical level.

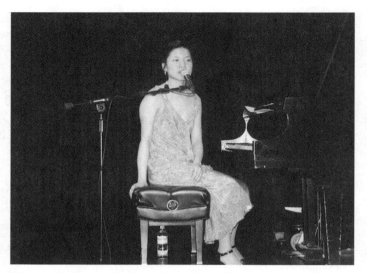

FIG. 4.1. Pianist and Composer Beata Moon Gives an Interactive Performance. Photo courtesy of Beata Moon.

If this pianist decides to explore consonance and dissonance through the analogy of tension and release, she will connect her listeners metaphorically. By offering a familiar parallel to the purely musical concept, a sophisticated musical entry point becomes accessible and understandable to a broad audience.

If her presentation includes a step where the listeners identify their own personal stresses and the ways they find relief, the entry point would connect the audience on a personal, emotional level.

A purely musical experience of an entry point enables the audience to listen actively like a musician. An intellectual or metaphorical experience of an entry point can universalize and demystify musical concepts. Personal, emotional encounters with entry points allow listeners to establish individual connections with the musical work.

"The most comprehensive interactions use entry points to connect the audience musically, intellectually, and emotionally."

The most comprehensive interactions use entry points to connect the audience musically, intellectually, and emotionally. The above pianist could address all three of these dimensions through the following multi-step activity:

1. Ask the audience to list common tensions in contemporary life and ways in which people find relief from them. Document the lists on a flipchart or a screen.
2. Get the audience to express items on the list by alternately sustaining and relaxing tension in various muscle groups.
3. Repeat the tension/release activity, but this time, accompany it with chords from Chopin's *Prelude in E minor, Op. 28 No. 4*.
4. Add a vocal element to the exercise by having the audience sing a sustained B while tensing and releasing muscles in response to how much tension they feel between their sung note and Chopin's piano chords.
5. Introduce and perform the prelude as the audience listens for musical tension and release.

Let's refer back to the revised *Also sprach Zarathustra* example from chapter 3 and see how it addresses all three dimensions of the entry point.

The basic idea behind the interaction was, "How does Richard Strauss use orchestration to convey a sense of spiritual awakening?" On a purely musical level, the entry point was orchestration. The audience was musically introduced to this entry point by hearing Strauss's instruments and themes in isolation. On a more metaphorical level, the audience listened for awakening and character. On a personal level, listeners had the opportunity to form their own individual interpretations of Strauss's orchestrated themes. The activity gave listeners three dimensions for connecting to the music, and they responded with enthusiasm.

Activities do not always need to include more than one way of connecting, but be intentional and strategic about how you are helping listeners to connect. To ensure your chosen entry point has the maximal effect, ask yourself: "How do I want the listener to relate to this piece?" "Am I connecting the listener musically?" "Is this abstract musical concept comprehensible?" "How can I make this music personally relevant?"

INTERACTIVE ARCHETYPES AND STRATEGIES

There are a myriad ways you can interact with your audiences. Following are many of the most common and effective archetypes for engaging your listeners. As you read, notice which strategies you tend to favor, and note new approaches you would like to try. You'll find quite a bit of information and ideas in this section, so take your time. You may find it helpful to revisit this chapter as you study the interactive concert transcripts in part iv.

Piece Simulation

In a piece simulation, you and your audience create or perform something analogous to the music they are about to hear.

Ensembles of many genres use piece simulations to sensitize audiences to syncopation, cross-rhythms, and the specific rhythmic roles of each musician. By dividing the audience into sections and having each player establish a rhythmic ostinato, very quickly, you can get an entire audience performing the composite rhythm of a piece. This is especially illuminating for music with many rhythmic layers, like Latin jazz, African drumming, tango, and classical chamber music.

Piece simulations can involve melody and other aspects of music as well. Before performing Heinrich Biber's *Passacaglia*, a solo violin work that consists of virtuosic variations over a repeated bass line (G-F-E♭-D), I like to create a passacaglia with the audience. I simply get them to sing Biber's bass line and improvise variations above it.

The logistics of these simulations will vary from piece to piece. The primary aim is to get the audience creating and performing something that is as much like the next work as possible. Doing so will cause them to listen with the insider perspective of a composer and performer. Because a piece simulation is one of the most powerful interactions, try to include one in every concert.

Listening Challenges and Activities

When you set up a piece, it is always helpful to give the audience a clear listening focus or challenge that stems from your entry point. The ideal listening assignments reward listeners in musically or personally significant ways. Counting how many times the bass line repeats in Pachelbel's *Canon in D* has little personal or musical value. A better approach would help listeners to hear how the lines develop, intensify, and follow one another in canon.

In preparing very young children (preschool through second grade) to hear an entirely instrumental jazz concert by the Lewis Nash Ensemble, teachers and I focused on the entry point of leadership, and how each member had a unique personality as an accompanist and soloist.

Over the course of preparatory workshops, students developed their abilities to listen with this mindset: "Who is the leader [soloist] now? How is he or she playing and moving? What is everyone else doing to help the leader?" As we reflected after the concert, they shared their observations and their questions ("How did they *know* who was the next leader?").

Sometimes, a listening assignment can be turned into a physical activity or game. At a Hudson Valley Philharmonic concert, audience members used hand signals to silently demonstrate their recognition of themes from Tchaikovsky's *Romeo and Juliet Fantasy Overture*. Listeners would put their hands over their hearts or make a fist, according to whether the orchestra was playing love themes or conflict themes.

Some conductors teach listeners to conduct along with a piece that has a strong metrical feel or widely contrasting dynamics. (And for a real kick, volunteers can be invited to conduct the orchestra in an encore of the work!)

Improvisation

Improvisation adds an air of excitement to a performance. Even musicians who do not consider themselves improvisers have effectively used improvisational techniques during an interactive concert. Following are a few ways that you can use improvisation:

1. Given a few parameters, volunteers from the audience can come onstage and improvise an instrumental or vocal solo. If you have a simple melody instrument like a xylophone, you can set it to a specific scale (e.g., the major pentatonic or the minor blues scale), taking away any extraneous notes. Usually, your volunteers will need one or two clear parameters (e.g., "Start slow, then get faster and faster," or "Start with low notes, and get higher and higher"). A little practice time also helps volunteers to succeed.

2. Performers can lead an improvisation that involves the whole audience in making music or sound. For instance, in concerts featuring the "Thunderstorm" movement from Beethoven's *Symphony No. 6*, performers have often led the audience in an improvised "thunderstorm" consisting of snapping, patting, stamping, and vocal sounds that approximate the dynamic changes of the symphony.

3. Some contemporary pieces include improvised parts for the audience or the musicians. Feel free to compose or commission new ones! Tania León and Thomas Cabaniss are two composers who have skillfully composed audience-participation into their works.

4. The musicians themselves can improvise, and the audience can coach them on their playing. At one Tanglewood Music Festival concert, a French horn player and a double bassist improvised a confrontational duet, which represented a battle between a hero and a villain.

5. Improvisation can also take the form of improvised movement, dance, or drama instead of music.

Improvisation provides unique opportunities for you and your audience to experiment with musical concepts and ideas. Exploring an entry point through spontaneous creation gives your audience a clearer picture of how the entry point functions than if you merely demonstrate it. Your audience will also have the satisfaction of participating in musical creation.

Composition

Effective composition activities are tricky within a concert setting, but with a little forethought, they can prove quite successful and musically revealing. Like improvisation, composition gives your audience the opportunity to manipulate musical materials. Composition opens up the creative process and can even result in music that closely resembles the works you are performing.

I once designed a concert entitled *Compose Yourself!*, a children's concert for the Bridgehampton Chamber Music Festival. Featuring a very young composer prodigy, Athena Adamopoulos, as my co-host, we taught children to listen for musical patterns and musical forms by teaching them the basic skills for creating them. Using voices and a xylophone, our listeners created melodies and short pieces in the forms of the pieces to be presented. The audience gained an active sense of how composers put pieces together, how the forms work, and how to *hear* them.

A few keys to making in-concert composition work:

1. Composition is a decision-making process, and an aesthetic one at that. If audiences are making random, unhearing decisions, they are not composing. You need to provide a clear framework for making aesthetic choices. ("So, here's the first note of our 'triumphant melody.' Do you want the next note to go up or down? Why? How far? Let me play you some options. . . . Let's vote on which one sounds most triumphant!")

2. In order to make melodic decisions, the audience needs a melodic tool. In addition to responding to a performer's demonstration of compositional choices, audiences can respond to visually structured instruments, such as the Chimalong metallophone, which has multicolored

pipes for distinguishing the various pitches. In effect, the audience can "compose by color." Of course, audiences can also express their melodic urges by humming or singing; the human voice is actually the best melodic tool of all.

If you can actually have a composer on stage to develop the audience's ideas at a piano or another instrument, you can create some really exciting stuff. For the Bridgehampton concert, Athena was able to develop the audience's ideas at the piano, showing the full range of possibility of each new idea. Commissioned pieces with pre-composed options (to be chosen by the audience at the performance) work well, too.

3. Tailor your parameters to the kind of piece you want. If you want to compose a singable, happy tune, the pentatonic major scale makes a great foundation. If you want to create dance music, choose an appropriate meter and tempo.

4. If you have enough musicians, you can break the audience into small groups and have one musician work with each group to create and interpret a newly composed piece of music.

5. One tactic that is always a hit at a community-based concert is to have people or children from the community compose a piece to be performed at the event. This will take considerable advance work on the part of teaching artists, but the payoff is well worth the effort. Helping ordinary people to compose is a whole book unto itself; stay tuned. . . .

> **CONSIDER THIS: ROCK THIS BITCH!**
>
> At a Ben Folds concert, a fan once shouted, "Rock this bitch!" Folds seized the moment and improvised a song on the spot. From that point forward, "Rock this Bitch" became a staple of his concerts. Each time, Folds composes and arranges a completely new rendition of the song as the audience watches.
>
> Find and compare a few videos of his "Rock this Bitch" performances. How might you create something similar in your concerts? How might you give the audience and the musicians more input and creative control?

Audience "Perform-Along"

In a "perform-along," the audience has a chance to perform with the musicians as they play. A real perform-along is more sophisticated than simply clapping the beat. Rather, the audience learns a part and performs it in response to visual or musical cues.

The New York Philharmonic has led "sing-alongs" where the audience performs the "Ode to Joy" from Beethoven's *Symphony No. 9* with the orchestra. For Carnegie Hall's Link-Up programs, participants learn instrumental and vocal parts in preparatory workshops to perform live with an orchestra. In lieu of preparatory workshops, simpler accompaniments and parts can be learned during a concert.

Of course, we have many precedents for "perform-alongs" outside of educational concerts. "*Messiah* sings" are a staple of December performance calendars around the world. Pete Seeger always got his audience singing, whether using a well-known tune, or masterfully teaching the audience a new song, even while he performs it. My personal favorite happened at a Juilliard Orchestra concert where Bobby McFerrin got an audience of a few thousand to sing Gounod's "Ave Maria" while he vocalized Bach's first prelude from *The Well-Tempered Clavier*.

One of the major achievements of "perform-alongs" is that they totally demolish the delineation between listeners and performers. For a moment, audience members enjoy the thrill of being equal partners with great musicians. What more could a music-lover want?

> **CONSIDER THIS: ANTHEMS**
>
> Across many genres, certain songs become anthems with fans. They know all the words to Ice Cube's "It Was a Good Day," or spontaneously join in with Bono's "How long?" when U2 sings "40."
> What potential "anthems" do you have in your repertoire? What opportunities do you have for a meaningful or unifying sing-along or perform-along?

Musician Coaching

The audience can coach performers on everything from mood to tempo to dynamics, and so on. A "musician coaching" pays the most dividends when tied to a specific, piece-related inquiry.

For instance, during a children's concert focused on "What makes music sound heroic?" a Hudson Valley Philharmonic trumpet player performed the fanfare from Rossini's *William Tell Overture* in a completely non-heroic way: he played the solo softly, smoothly, slowly, and in a minor key. The audience offered suggestions for making the solo more heroic until it finally became Rossini's original version. In another instance, an orchestra performed "Aquarium" from Camille Saint-Saëns' *Carnival of the Animals* in a very plain manner and took suggestions from the audience on how to give the music more of a "watery" feeling.

Audience members enjoy making interpretive decisions about how a piece will be performed. Try letting them tinker with dynamics, tempo, and other musical aspects.

Musician Audition

Sometimes in an interactive performance, musicians can audition for a particular improvisational or musical role. At a New York Philharmonic Young People's concert, prior to a performance of Aaron Copland's "Variations on a Shaker Melody" from *Appalachian Spring*, the audience and orchestra created their own original variation on Copland's theme. As part of the process, various instruments auditioned to perform the melody and accompaniment parts.

At a Tanglewood Family Concert, musicians turned an audition into a competition: they tried to see who could sound the most like a bug. The winner had the dubious distinction of being swallowed by a "frog" instrument in an improvisation. The orchestra segued to Rimsky-Korsakov's *Flight of the Bumblebee*, and other buggy selections.

Bands can use a similar process to create a fresh new arrangement with the audience. Who gets to sing lead vocals or harmony? Who gets to solo?

Visual Activities/Visual Aids

Because many people are primarily visual, it is important to find ways to include visual elements in your interactive performance. How might you use lighting, projections, or video to enhance the musical experience? How might dress or costuming play a role? Visual aids and props are helpful, but they are most effective when performers use them in active ways that reflect or respond to musical content.

Watching something analogous to the music can help to focus listeners' ears. While light shows, video, or projections have become mandatory for high-end stadium concerts, we can also use lower-tech, but effective visual connections in venues of smaller scale.

At one Hudson Valley Philharmonic children's concert, a huge gray tarpaulin helped people to notice the many varieties of musical waves that Felix Mendelssohn creates in *The Hebrides* overture, which depicts a rolling, stormy sea. Volunteers from the audience came forward and shook the tarpaulin to simulate ocean waves that corresponded to orchestral excerpts demonstrating Mendelssohn's different wave intensities.

Multimedia

I once attended a concert at the Brooklyn Academy of Music entitled *A Magic Science: Celebrating Jimi Hendrix*. A diverse array of musical artists including Vernon Reid; Medeski, Martin, and Wood; Sandra St. Victor; and members of the Gil Evans Orchestra reinterpreted classic Jimi Hendrix songs through various contemporary genres.

Among the stars of the evening was Glenn McKay, one of the originators of psychedelic liquid light shows, who made his name touring with Jefferson Airplane and lighting many shows at the Fillmore in San Francisco. McKay's projections unified the evening, as he spontaneously projected colors that pulsed and connected intuitively with the sounds and rhythms of each song.

Recently, orchestras and other performing arts organizations have begun to make more use of technology, lighting, and multimedia in concert situations. Concert pianist Bruce Brubaker sometimes makes subtle, innovative use of colored lighting effects in his concerts and recitals, as does the new music chamber orchestra Absolute Ensemble.

Carnegie Hall's educational programs deserve special recognition for their successful use of listening maps, animated icons, and projections to help listeners follow musical themes and forms.[3] Without a doubt, multimedia has incredible potential, and new possibilities are on the horizon.

But before we get overexcited and spend vast sums of money on the latest computerized lighting, projection, and animation systems, we should be clear on one thing: *multimedia is only beneficial to the extent it enhances the listening or artistic experience.* Often, in a well-intentioned attempt to dazzle ticket buyers, multimedia efforts end up creating expensive, unnecessary, and unhelpful distractions. In order for multimedia to be effective, it must do something for our ears and minds.

I took my first real plunge into the realm of multimedia when I created a slideshow for the Hudson Valley Philharmonic's performance of Bedrich Smetana's tone poem *Vltava (The Moldau),* which depicts a journey from the source of a river to its mouth. As the river flows, it passes hunters, a wedding, a moonlit scene, rapids, a castle, and so forth. The work was performed twelve times as part of a young people's concert tour for thousands of school children.

As a visual analogue to Smetana's journey, the slideshow took us on a parallel journey from the headwaters of the Hudson River to its mouth in Hudson Bay. For every six seconds of music, I painstakingly chose an appropriate slide to correspond to Smetana's imagery and orchestration.

---

3. Visit www.carnegiehall.org for online examples.

At the concerts, the elementary and middle school audience listened attentively for the work's duration. Given the work's more than ten-minute duration, many would consider this a great success. That said, I noticed that I personally did not listen quite as deeply as when there were no images. For better or for worse, visual images do sap quite a bit of our attention. If we aren't careful, multimedia efforts can relegate music to a background role, and listening can become more passive.

I do believe that the slide show had musical integrity, and according to many teacher evaluations, it helped visually oriented audience members to maintain their focus. However, given our art form's aural nature and our culture's overreliance on visual stimuli, I would not advocate relying exclusively on this kind of approach.

Another danger of multimedia is that it increases one's susceptibility to Murphy's Law. At one of the shows, our slide projector mysteriously became unplugged, and we heard Smetana's piece without visuals. I was relieved to notice that the listeners were still able to focus on the music, since the orchestra had demonstrated themes from the different sections beforehand.

Interdisciplinary Approaches

Musicians have become increasingly involved in collaborating with choreographers, filmmakers, actors, storytellers, and other artists. Of particular note are Yo-Yo Ma's *Inspired by Bach* interdisciplinary explorations of J.S. Bach's cello suites, which aired on PBS television.

FIG. 4.2. Cellist Yo-Yo Ma Collaborates with Pipa Player Wu Man in the New York Philharmonic's *A Silk Road to China* Interactive Concert. Photo Credit: Michael DiVito.

Chicago's *Fifth House Ensemble*, an enterprising chamber group, engages theater groups, visual artists, animators, folk musicians, rock bands, and living composers to create interdisciplinary thematic performances that provide deep encounters with established and new repertoire. Other companies such as composer Paola Prestini's VisionIntoArt, develop completely original interdisciplinary creations involving art, dance, music, poetry, and film.

The rewards of collaboration are many, and if all artists strive to give the audience entry points into one another's art works, amazing and aesthetic experiences will follow.

Of course, it is possible to include an interdisciplinary approach for just one piece or segment of a concert as well. As with multimedia, keep an eye out for maintaining musical integrity. Constantly ask yourself, "Does this serve the music? Does this enhance the hearing of this piece?" or "Is this a satisfying work of art unto itself?"

> **CONSIDER THIS: MULTIMEDIA COLLABORATORS**
>
> Who are some artists outside of your own discipline who might be able to contribute something unique to your performance? Who are some collaborative artists who might enrich your own creative process or performances?

Using One Performance as a "Warm-Up" for the Next Work

Sometimes, one musical performance can sharpen the listeners' perceptions of a work that follows. A televised Boston Pops concert presented an extraordinary example of this approach. Prior to a performance of a movement from Igor Stravinsky's *The Rite of Spring*, two guest musicians from the Broadway musical *Stomp* were invited to the stage.

Dressed in garbage can lids and other household objects, the guest artists performed a stunning, polyrhythmic percussion duet that was as gymnastic as it was musical. Striking themselves and each other, they built their performance to a thrillingly complex, cacophonous climax. The duet sensitized listeners to rhythm, accents, and sheer unbridled energy. When the orchestra segued to Stravinsky's dance, any listener would hear the raw, visceral, rhythmic power like never before. The performers from *Stomp* had prepared us to receive the full impact and vitality of Stravinsky's shocking and invigorating music.

Offering the Audience a Second Helping

Most musicians agree that multiple hearings facilitate deeper understanding of musical works. I am grateful for a recital in which the Muir String Quartet performed Anton Webern's *Six Bagatelles* both before and after intermission. The first hearing familiarized me with Webern's delicate timbres and surprising economy of form; the second hearing allowed me to concentrate more fully on Webern's motives and phrasing.

Second hearings are most helpful for illuminating sophisticated pieces. Any piece that does not reveal all of its treasures on one hearing makes a good candidate for a repeat performance. By offering multiple hearings, you can give the audience the opportunity to listen to a particular piece in different ways.

Similarly, bands and singers will occasionally reprise a song or a chorus during the course of an evening, because the intervening words and music provide a new context and meaning for the second hearing.

In interactive performances, we can provide strategic opportunities for the audience to hear works more than once. I once began a family concert with the musicians entering and performing the opening *Allegro* from a harpsichord concerto by J.S. Bach. After performing other works and leading several activities that heightened the audience's sense of counterpoint and phrase structure, the musicians repeated the *Allegro* as their finale. The audience was hearing in such a focused way that some listeners said it almost sounded like a different piece. In actuality, the first performance helped listeners to digest the "big picture" of the movement. The intervening activities prepared listeners to notice the details.

Taking Requests

Honoring audience requests is a time-honored way of establishing an in-the-moment connection with your audience. In many cases, these requests come from fans who know and love your best work. While a certain number of requests may naturally arise, you can also consciously build this engagement opportunity into your events.

Two hours into a concert, Bruce Springsteen goes out into the stadium crowd and takes the audience's song requests, which they offer on hand-drawn posters. For the next forty-five minutes, the audience determines the set list.

Dialogue-Based Activities

Speaking is probably the most common form of interaction between musicians and their audiences. We should always look for ways to open the dialogue up further. Some musicians are fond of going out into their audiences to interview people or converse with them. If you have a philosophical question to pose to the audience, you can take a moment to have the audience "talk amongst themselves" and then share their conclusions with the large group. When using dialogue, keep it creative, and give the audience input when you can.

> *"Speaking is probably the most common form of interaction between musicians and their audiences. We should always look for ways to open the dialogue up further."*

The contemporary music group Eighth Blackbird sometimes structures their dialogues in ways that illumine the work they are about to perform. For instance, a rondo movement might be preceded by a spoken introduction in rondo form.

Use of Underscoring, Voiceover, and Narrative

Having musicians underscore spoken sections of your program can be an effective way of keeping the momentum moving forward, or to provide punctuation for a free-styling storyteller. For many superlative examples, notice how George Clinton exhorts his audiences or introduces members of Parliament-Funkadelic over a funk vamp. Trace Clinton's approach to the source: the declamatory tradition of gospel ministers and singers. Watch Pastor Shirley Caesar and Donny McClurkin as they perform for a church service, and notice how they and their musicians hold an audience's attention as they deliver a message and introduce a song.

Underscoring can allow artists the opportunity to share quite extensive stories that otherwise would be too long for maintaining musical momentum. Yet, the time invested can really highlight the next selection.

David Lee Roth's concert introduction to Van Halen's rockabilly song "Ice Cream Man" provides an excellent study in how an underscored introduction can strengthen the impact of a song. In fact, though this is the only song from Van Halen's debut album that wasn't released as a single, Roth's storytelling approach elevated it to become one of their concert staples.

Over the years, Roth developed an extensive introduction in which he plays blues harmonica and slide guitar as he lazily improvises a nostalgic tale—usually about a high-school friend who actually drove an ice cream truck and the parties that ensued. In addition to setting the mood and building the audience's and band's connection to the song, the slow, musically free nature of Roth's intro creates a radical contrast with the up-tempo, hard-rocking song, once it comes.

Voiceovers can also be used selectively during a performance to highlight the music. Sigurd Barrett, star of long-running Danish music education television show *Sigurd og Symfoniorkestret*, often includes a storytelling voiceover to an instrumental classical composition. At a concert in Aalborg, I witnessed how Sigurd's co-host, Nikolaj Hansen sporadically interwove lines describing a benign morning in the life of a caterpillar over a composition by Maurice Ravel. The tale extended toddlers' attention spans while letting the music stay in the foreground.

Of course, when using this approach, we definitely run the risk of superimposing extra-musical interpretations that were not what the composer of the music intended. On the other hand, sometimes we can use a voiceover that directly ties to programmatic content.

For many years, I've served on the faculty of MWROC, a rock festival directed by Mark Wood. One year, Chuck Bontrager was performing one of my solo instrumental metal compositions, *Nahum: An Apocalyptic Prophesy for Electric Violin or Viola*, a work inspired by an ancient Hebrew prophesy of doom.

Chuck requested that I recite lines from the prophesy as a voiceover during the piece's slow introduction. I took selected lines that summarized the essence of the prophesy and wove them as counterpoint to Chuck's musical phrases. A musician in attendance who knew the work well mentioned that the effect was riveting, and possibly her favorite performance of the work.

Demonstration

While not necessarily interactive in and of itself, demonstrating musical ideas and themes can be enormously helpful to listeners. Usually, a savvy performer can find ways to enhance the demonstration through audience participation. If audiences can perform or manipulate the material being demonstrated, they will be even more likely to recognize it when they listen to the performance.

An audience can usually be taught a melody or a rhythm through a call-and-response process. When teaching melodies and rhythms, adding physical gestures to the singing (such as tracing the highs and lows of melodic contours with the hands) can prove helpful to kinesthetic and visual learners. Sometimes, examples are perceived more clearly if the demonstration initially happens slower than the performance tempo.

Keep all demonstrations concise, yet substantial enough to be processed and remembered.

Games

Games can provide a fun way to illumine the music. A string quintet from the Manhattan School of Music once used "musical charades" to put a puzzle-solving spin on Camille Saint-Saëns' *Carnival of the Animals*. Listeners had to use musical clues to determine what animal the different instruments were depicting.

The New York Philharmonic Teaching Artist Ensemble invoked *Sesame Street's* "one of these things is not like the others" game to highlight how one instrument plays in a totally different key in a movement of Igor Stravinsky's *Petrouchka*. Simon Says, Follow the Leader, Twenty Questions, Truth or Dare, and other games can easily be exploited in concerts for children, as well as for adults. Make a list of fun games, and keep it handy.

> **CONSIDER THIS: THE REMOTE CONTROL GAME**
>
> Cellist Wendy Law of *Classical Jam* and *Voxare Quartet* invented "The Remote Control Game," a powerful audience-engagement technique that has been widely adapted and copied. In its original form, the activity was designed to highlight the widely contrasting instrumental roles in the fourth movement of Erwin Schulhoff's *Concertino for Flute, Viola, and Double Bass*.
>
> Wendy gave a volunteer from the audience a "magical" remote control, which could mute or unmute musicians. (When muted, the musicians would pantomime playing and rejoin when unmuted.) An extraordinarily fun activity that really helps listeners to identify and isolate the musical roles of different musicians, other ensembles and conductors have adapted and expanded the game, sometimes using the remote to cue melodies or improvisation.

Puzzles or Problems to Solve

Everybody likes mysteries, riddles, and puzzles. One group of Manhattan School of Music students created an educational concert with a *Mission: Impossible* theme. Each musician portrayed a secret agent who was given a paper with a secret mission or mystery to solve. The audience helped each agent with his or her assignment. Listeners learned musical concepts through problem-solving and discovery instead of didactic explanations. Of course, having each message self-destruct with the help of combustible flash-paper didn't hurt the entertainment value of their presentation!

Other Archetypes

The above list of activity types is by no means comprehensive! Continue to observe and categorize activities, and create new ways to connect to your audience. Be sure to share them with the rest of us!

Application

Choose a work or two that you or your ensemble is performing in concert. Go through the interactive archetypes, and design a few different activities that could be used in a concert setting. Try them out. Which seems to be most effective in focusing the audience on the music?

PART II
Deeper and Better Engagement

CHAPTER 5

Developing an Engaging Stage Presence

The instant we interact with an audience, we enter the theatrical realm. Surprised?

I was.

Because I learned about music from lectures, lessons, and master classes, my role models for presenting music were professors and teachers. The minute I stepped into a middle-school auditorium, I suddenly realized that gifted presenters rely on much more than rote skills and a thorough knowledge of their subject matter. I became acutely aware that the most engaging speakers possess a wonderful sense of theatricality and drama, as well as a capacity to receive verbal and non-verbal feedback from their audiences.

> *"Even if we aren't in the running for an Oscar or a Tony, we should still strive to make our events theatrically engaging."*

Even if we aren't in the running for an Oscar or a Tony, we should still strive to make our events theatrically engaging. Our decisions about venue, set, lighting, blocking (stage movement), props, and speaking should incline an audience to stay with the music and work harder as a listener.

Your choice of a performance space sets the tone for the event. If you are planning a fully interactive concert with considerable audience participation, a large concert hall may not be the most conducive environment.

Adopt a broad view of what constitutes a performance space. You really can play anywhere you like. These days, professional musical performances happen at art galleries, factories, golf courses, microbreweries, train stations, supermarkets, church fellowship halls, apartment building rooftops, fitness centers and gyms, Boys' and Girls' Clubs, nightclubs, town squares, children's museums, prisons, music shops, barns, comedy clubs, furniture stores, retirement homes, bookstores, backyards, hotel ballrooms, psychiatric wards, country clubs, hospitals, orphanages, libraries, firehouses, campgrounds, and other great places.

Oftentimes, you can partner with a business or organization that will provide space, sponsorship, discount catering, or other services in exchange for advertising and the customer-drawing power of your presence.

Whatever your venue, consider ways in which you can use and set the space in inviting and provocative ways. I once attended a concert by the microtonal ensemble Newband, which was performing in a small stone cathedral in Brooklyn. Upon entering the church, people encountered a sanctuary that was pitch dark, save for a blue-lit menagerie of bizarre-looking instruments built by iconoclastic American composer Harry Partch. Giant-sized marimbas, kitharas resembling ancient Greek altars, and glass domes suspended like jellyfish from chains created an expectation of something ancient, contemporary, dramatic, and extraordinary.

FIG. 5.1. Newband Performing in the 2005 Production of *Oedipus* by Harry Partch at Montclair State University's Alexander Kasser Theater. Photo credit: Mike Peters.

The band itself demonstrated substantial theatrical savvy. Wearing austere, mostly black attire, the musicians entered the hall from the back, solemnly proceeding down the aisle in pairs. Once onstage, they judiciously avoided dark or unlit spaces and remained in the light. When performing, they "cheated to the audience" by keeping their bodies and faces turned towards us, even when looking sideways or turning pages. Consequently, it felt like they were always directing all of their energy and music towards us. When performers assumed the occasional speaking or singing role, their steady, varied eye contact made the whole audience feel acknowledged.

At intermission, the house lights went up, and the audience was invited to walk around the performance space to take a closer look at Partch's magnificent contraptions. A stage diagram and instrument guide in the program gave us the name, materials, and history of each instrument.

When the house dimmed again, the blue lighting gels had been switched to amber ones to give the impression of natural sunlight. To our surprise, instead of another procession or a conventional entrance from backstage, the performers ambled in from all areas of the church. Dressed like down-and-out itinerants from John Steinbeck's *The Grapes of Wrath* and wearing makeup that gave the appearance of dirt, grease smears, and five o'clock shadows, they limped and hobbled up to us and hoarsely whispered, "Spare a dime, mister?. . . Spare change, ma'am?" Gradually finding their way to their instruments, they commenced Partch's *U.S. Highball,* an epic operatic chronicle of American hobo life during the Great Depression. Remarkably, the instrumentalists who had looked so contemporary and angular before continued to play with intensity and precision while projecting the loose, lazy, and sardonic body language appropriate for Partch's libretto.

Had Newband omitted its numerous theatrical touches, the evening still would have been a musically satisfying concert. However, the ensemble's careful planning and attention to matters of set, lighting, staging, body English, dress, speech, and presentation made the event an electrifying experience I can vividly recall decades later.

> **CONSIDER THIS: THEATRICAL THINKING**
>
> The following checklist of questions can help to stimulate theatrical thinking as you plan the presentational aspects of your performance:
>
> - How could we set the stage in evocative or inviting ways that relate to our theme? How could we use lighting to enhance the concert?
> - What props might we use?
> - What kind of dress do we want? If we were to use costumes, what might we wear?
> - At what points can we make creative entrances or exits? When might we go out into the audience?
> - What is our plan for moving about onstage? How can we make use of the whole stage or the entire hall? Are there instances where the musicians could move while they are performing?
> - What kind of language do we want to use? (Formal, informal, bilingual, Shakespearean. . . .) What manner of speaking is best suited to our audience and our theme?
> - Are there points in our program where we might include actors, dancers, poets, or other kinds of artists?
> - What can the musicians or ensemble do to enhance their stage presence?
> - How can we achieve dramatic effects with the musical selections? Can we have the music begin suddenly or in unexpected ways? Could we put performers in the house?

We need to be just as aware of these presentational aspects when planning our own concerts. For theatrical elements to be effective in a concert, they must be intentional and professional. While some musicians have a natural theatrical flair, anyone can benefit from the insight of a drama coach or producer. Expert input can significantly increase confidence and presentational quality, so seriously consider contacting a professional coach or producer.

Even with professional guidance, we would do well to increase our awareness of two key areas of our presentation: speech and movement.

SPEAKING

As with performing a piece of music, it's not necessarily what you say, it's how you say it. We all know that we should project from our diaphragms and speak clearly, evenly, and with appropriate spirit. We know not to mumble, rush our words, look at our feet or the ceiling. We know that reading our lines from a script usually makes for an awkward presentation. In addition to those familiar shortcomings, I have observed a few subtler gaffes to avoid.

> *"As with performing a piece of music, it's not necessarily what you say, it's how you say it."*

Sometimes, musicians inadvertently turn their backs to their audience while speaking, and the audience misses the last part of what is being said. Seems odd? It usually happens when musicians are getting ready to play the next piece. In an effort to keep things moving, they move to get their instruments while they are finishing a spoken introduction.

To avoid showing the audience your backside, simply finish what you have to say and take the necessary five seconds to get your instrument and your bearings. The audience has a much shorter wait than it feels like onstage.

A related mistake is failing to stay on mic. In many situations, we will use microphones for speaking to our audiences and to ensure a strong audio signal for a recording, live-stream, or broadcast. If you are using a microphone, be sure that all of your and your colleagues' speaking is on mic. If we get too casual about speaking to our audiences off mic, not everyone will hear what is being said.

Wait until the applause has died down to start speaking. When we don't, our first sentence or so is unintelligible. Again, this impulse usually comes from a healthy urge to keep the momentum going.

If you are concerned about people losing focus during a lengthy ovation, you can gently give the audience a cutoff signal, or a "Thank You!" For certain classical or liturgical situations, you can simply ask that applause be withheld until the program's conclusion.

In addition to avoiding detrimental habits, we can consciously use some effective speaking strategies. A positive technique to add to your verbal kitbag is "ping-ponging." When sharing the stage with other speakers, take turns frequently—even within a paragraph. Changing speakers holds the audience's attention, and they are less prone to "space out" during verbal sections of your presentation. What works for morning television news also works for the stage.

Economize your words. One clear image is worth paragraphs of description. Effective metaphors and questions are golden. Include humor when appropriate.

"Economize your words."

Avoid being overly formulaic about providing a spoken setup and then having the musicians get ready and begin. There is good theatrical impact when music comes in dramatically, surprisingly, or in conjunction with verbal pauses. Consider how you plan to use silence in your performance. In addition to moments where silence may have a theatrical impact, silence can set up a discipline for listening to music.

MOVEMENT AND STAGE PRESENCE

Again, we know that we shouldn't pace, fidget, gesture excessively, or be a stiff. Nevertheless, we all have habits and mannerisms, good and bad. Watch a video of one of your interactive performances. Give yourself due credit, as well as critique. Document what you learn, and set presentational goals for your next performance.

Application

For years, Concert Artists Guild hired Janet Bookspan, a remarkable stage director, drama coach, actress, and musician to groom its competition winners for their community concerts and general presentation skills. Let's try one of her tried-and-true stage presence exercises.

Stand in the middle of a modest-sized room. Center yourself: feet under hips, hips under shoulders, weight evenly distributed and balanced between both feet. Shift your weight back and forth a bit until everything is balanced. Make sure that your knees and hips are flexible and unlocked.

Once you have found your center and balance, close your eyes. Sense the space around you, including the walls and the ceiling. Slowly imagine that your body is expanding. Feel as though your feet are sinking into the ground, while your torso and neck release, lengthening and widening. Sense that your arms are lengthening until they feel long enough to touch the walls. Allow your spine and neck to release and expand until your rising head feels like it can touch the ceiling. Once you feel like you've filled the space, with your head reaching the ceiling and your hands long enough to touch the walls, open your eyes. Enjoy occupying the full space with your full size. Move to a larger room and repeat the exercise. Keep practicing with larger and larger spaces.

With practice, you will be able to quickly embody your full size and project your energy and presence in any space or performance venue. I still do this exercise just before walking onstage.

In addition to monitoring and refining your own stage habits, start to imagine ways that you can add theatrical class to your presentations. Look for creative ways to use or enhance the performance space. Consider going into the house during the performance or making an unusual entrance or exit.[4] Be aware of your light, body position, and eye contact with the audience. No matter what repertoire you are performing, the audience always appreciates a good show.

Remember that every moment you are on stage, you are a presence on the stage. If you are performing, perform passionately. If you are sitting as another musician speaks, presents, or performs, give her your attention and focus. This will help the audience to focus.

---

4. World-class percussion soloist Evelyn Glennie wins the prize for "most theatrical entrance" for entering through the back of Avery Fisher Hall, chanting electronically-manipulated alien vocal sounds, bowing an ethereal sounding instrument called a "waterphone," and wearing a silver, spandex spacesuit when performing Michael Daugherty's *UFO* with the New York Philharmonic.

If you are hosting, but not playing, what you do when the musicians perform can still have a major impact on the audience. When Jon Deak, associate principal double bass of the New York Philharmonic, hosts a Young People's Concert, he listens in ways that guide the listener.

FIG. 5.2. Jon Deak Hosting a New York Philharmonic Young People's Concert. Photo credit: Michael DiVito.

His head punctuates the rhythms we hear; his body leans towards the instruments with the primary line; his facial expressions respond to the mood of the music. Jon is not following a choreographed routine; he is responding naturally to the music he hears. But he communicates his listening experience in such clear and visual ways that the audience can't help but respond sympathetically.

When you have the role of listening host or colleague, think about how you can model listening for your audience. If the music is a style that invites shouts, cheers, applause, or an "Amen!," set an enthusiastic example for the audience! If the scenario is more formal, position yourself in a way that doesn't distract. Some musicians prefer to listen from the side of the stage; others take a slightly off-center or below-the-stage position. If you are in clear view, try adjusting your chair or stool so that your body is at an angle to the musicians and the audience. This way, you can alternately turn your focus towards the musicians or the listeners.

"If the music is a style that invites shouts, cheers, applause, or an "Amen!," set an enthusiastic example for the audience! "

Take the time to plan and polish the presentational parts of your performance. You will gain confidence and finesse, and your audience will notice.

> **CONSIDER THIS: DEVELOPING YOUR PHYSICAL PRESENCE**
>
> As a new graduate student, I learned a powerful stage presence exercise from my viola teacher, Karen Ritscher. One day, Karen said, "You know, David, I wouldn't know just from looking at you that you're as good of a player as you are. Let's work on developing a strong, commanding physical presence."
>
> "This week go walk the New York City sidewalks and confidently keep saying to yourself, *'I'm David Wallace!'* Take up as much space on the sidewalk as you can. Resist the urge to close yourself off, and don't let other people push you out of the way. Keep smiling and confidently thinking, *'I'm David Wallace!'* If you bear yourself well, other people will make room for you. *They'll* be the ones who get out of your way. Stay physically open, and set your own tempo. Once you've got the hang of it, see if you can actually make eye contact or engage others. Elicit some smiles and nods. *'I'm David Wallace!'*"
>
> That week, the bustling Broadway sidewalks taught me more about how to comport myself than I could have imagined possible. Go practice your stage presence and confidence on a busy city sidewalk, or in a shopping mall, a grocery store, an airport check-in line, or a crowded school hallway. Occupy your full space and rightful place. Move at your own tempo, and confidently tell yourself, *"I'm [insert your full name here]!"*

CHAPTER 6

Avoiding Ten Common Pitfalls

So far, we've discussed how to use interactive performance strategies to enliven and deepen an audience's concert experience. In theory, we know what to do. Now, let's learn what *not* to do!

The following pitfalls appear again and again in my field observations, coaching sessions, and even my own concert-planning process. Unfortunately, these tendencies tend to resurface whenever we design new programs because we are bucking bad habits, long traditions, and entrenched ways of thinking. The good news is, we can avoid or correct each of these shortcomings with a little conscientious awareness and a good dose of musical integrity.

PITFALL 1: TOO MANY WORDS

In the Talking Heads song "Psycho Killer," David Byrne famously gibes, "You're talking a lot, but you're not saying anything!" When describing unsatisfying interactive performances, audiences most commonly complain, "The performers just rambled on and on," or "The language was too technical and difficult to understand." Both of these errors can be avoided in the scripting phase.

Effective scriptwriting focuses our speech by limiting and refining our words. A first complete draft will likely have sections that are too long or too verbose. When revising a first draft, try giving yourself the objective of reducing the total number of words by one third.

Look for wordy passages and scrutinize them. Are you saying only what is necessary? Are you clear and focused in how you say it? Can you break this passage up with illustrative musical examples or participatory moments? Speaking the text aloud or reading it to a friend will help you tremendously. Occasionally, I'll even run a script through a speech synthesis application. If a script makes sense when read in a computerized monotone, it's in good shape!

Once your script is concise and eloquent, it's time to check for unnecessary or unexplained technical information and jargon. Although we can do the troubleshooting ourselves, it's helpful to hand the script over to a non-musician. An objective reader or listener can easily tell when we are speaking in "insider language" or making little sense about complicated matters.

For fun, see if you can minimize or eliminate speaking components altogether. The first time I designed an interactive concert, my advising professor, Dr. Edward Bilous, challenged my group to create an audience-participatory concert that had absolutely no speaking until the post-performance reflection. The task seemed impossible and even crazy at first, but we met the challenge through creative improvisations, non-verbal communication, the incorporation of a goofy, clowning character, and a few posters. We were amazed by how deeply musicians could engage their audiences without saying a word.

PITFALL 2: DEMONSTRATION IN LIEU OF DISCOVERY

Did you ever have a literature teacher ruin a poem by analyzing it to death? Literary analysis can be a wonderful thing, but when an expert spoils our opportunity to explore a poem for ourselves, we become disenchanted. In a similar vein, concerts that rely too heavily on passive demonstrations can defeat their purpose by "telling all" in a way that sucks the life out of the music.

Many performances are one or two interactive steps shy of a mind-blowing experience. I recently saw a youth concert that had a solid theme, coherent script, and wonderful programming. The host and narrator presented the music with clarity and enthusiasm. He even articulated a specific listening focus for every work on the program. However, because everything was done in a presentational rather than a participatory fashion, the audience was not as musically engaged or enthusiastic as they might have been. Because we had no hands-on experiences of the entry points, we became passive listeners who (at most) heard only what we were told to hear.

I once coached a Juilliard student string quartet that was preparing to give an interactive performance of George Crumb's *Black Angels: Thirteen Images from the Dark Land*, an intense, contemporary work for amplified string quartet.

In the third movement, Crumb gets unusual sounds by having the quartet play their instruments with glass rods, thimbles, and paperclips. To complete his exotic and evocative sonic palette, some musicians also bow tam-tams (gongs) and water-filled crystal goblets. These combined techniques fill the air with eerie, unexpected, and otherworldly textures.

At the dress rehearsal, the group meticulously demonstrated all of Crumb's sounds. The demonstrations were clear and concise, but somehow, when the movement was finally played, the unusual techniques lost their edge. Ironically, the audience knew what was coming too well, so the music no longer surprised or excited us. The quartet realized it had to roll up its sleeves and find a way to familiarize the audience with the objects and their potential timbres, without spoiling Crumb's intrigue.

The group devised a new, inquiry-based strategy that allowed the audience to experiment with the unusual objects. Each quartet member would hold up one of the objects and let the audience give suggestions on how the item might be used to make "sounds from a dark land" with or without his or her instrument. Instead of being passive recipients of information, the audience members would now be wearing George Crumb's shoes as an expressive sound-explorer.

At the performance, listeners were fascinated as each musician tried out the suggestions, many of which proved humorous and challenging. Following this experiment, the audience was primed for the quartet's listening challenge: "Now let's see and hear how George Crumb creates dark sounds and images with these items!"

This time, as the group performed, Crumb's effects revealed themselves in the moment. The audience was pleased to recognize many of their own techniques, but they were also surprised by novel ideas they had not considered.

The quality of the quartet's performance was just as fine in the dress rehearsal, but this time, the audience's experience was vastly different. Why? People were now listening with the mindset, "What happens next?!" instead of "We already know what happens next." Whereas the dress-rehearsal audience had listened as knowledgeable but passive individuals, the concert audience listened as Crumb's sound-exploring colleagues. The latter group fully understood his delight in creating weird sounds with unusual objects. The moral? Inquiry-based discovery proves much more effective than passive demonstration.

> *"Inquiry-based discovery proves much more effective than passive demonstration."*

PITFALL 3: UNDER-REHEARSED LINES

Sadly, many otherwise brilliant concerts suffer from verbal stumbling, delayed responses to spoken cues, or on-stage confusion about what comes next. In most cases, the performances could have achieved their full potential with an extra run-through and a few additional hours of oral rehearsal.

As performers, we dedicate thousands of hours of our lives to practicing our instruments and perfecting the music we perform. We naturally hold ourselves to high playing standards. Our dedication to our craft is laudable, but we often forget that the audience holds us to presentational standards that are equally high.

Rehearse your script more than you think is necessary. Strive for tight cueing, excitingly crisp back-and-forth between words and music, clarity of focus, and a sense of precision throughout the performance. If there are technical details like lighting or miking, rehearse those aspects as well. I have never seen a concert where the presentational aspects seemed "over-prepared."

> *"Rehearse your script more than you think is necessary. I have never seen a concert where the presentational aspects seemed 'over-prepared.'"*

During the final rehearsal before a school tour, the bass player of a Manhattan School of Music group paused and said, "You know, this movement wasn't quite together. I feel like we really need to spend the rest of our rehearsal time going over the music."

As the ensemble's coach, the last thing I wanted to do was discourage musical rehearsal, but time and again, I had seen excellent musicianship undermined by sloppy or inadequate stage presentation.

"Mark, I appreciate your impulse to make the concert as musically solid as possible, but I have to tell you that the performance you just gave would knock the socks off of any fourth-grader in New York City. However, if you fumble your words, our group won't command the respect and attention it deserves. Every day, those fourth-graders watch polished actors and speakers on television, and like it or not, that's the standard they'll apply to your spoken dialogue. Unless you think the group's speaking is ready to hold its own against Hollywood's best, I think we should keep working on presentation."

After a thoughtful pause, Mark and the others agreed. For the record, the group scheduled an additional rehearsal to refine the music and run the script one more time. At the concert, the audience was rapt.

PITFALL 4: UNDER-REHEARSED MUSIC

Although we musicians usually hold ourselves to high performance standards, too often, family concerts, school concerts, and community engagement events suffer from embarrassing mistakes and sloppy musical execution.

Why do we fall short of our usual standards? The reason generally boils down to one of two fundamental issues:

- Organizations are unwilling or unable to compensate us for the necessary rehearsal time, so we give priority to more profitable or higher-profile endeavors.
- We, or our employers, have a philosophically flawed view about the general significance of community engagement and interactive performance.

What do I mean by a philosophically flawed view? Like the rest of the world, today's music scene still suffers from an unspoken hierarchy where the significance of a performance or a performer is based upon earnings, fame, venue, and publicity.

A few decades ago, when performing arts organizations and patrons concluded that musicians should present their music to communities, schools, and underserved populations (because "it's a nice thing to do; there's grant money for it, and musicians need to develop future audiences"), the added performances were perceived as something extra, or something that musicians had to do, like it or not. Outreach performances became regarded in the same light as spinach: healthful, but not necessarily tasty.

Some performers even regarded interactive performance as work that musicians do until they become professionally established enough that they don't have to bother with it anymore.

Categorizing performances as "those that matter much" and "those that matter less" is a flawed and artless approach to music-making. People attend concerts because they expect to receive and appreciate the performers' gifts. Offering them anything less than our finest work is selfish and rude.

Believe it or not, an untrained audience *can* sense the difference between a good performance and a great one. Listeners may not be able to articulate the difference, but they definitely know and appreciate when performers deliver their absolute best. They also can tell the difference between a performance that the musicians are genuinely delighted to give, and one in which the players are going through the motions with a smile on their faces (or not).

More than likely, you will have at least one pair of highly discriminating ears in every audience. Once after a very low-profile performance, a listener shook my hand and exclaimed, "That was great!" A mutual friend introduced him as international violin soloist and recording artist Gil Shaham. I'm glad that I was on my toes that day.

Whenever we walk off the stage, we should feel like we've given our best effort, no matter who's listening or whether or not we are paid. Since you're taking the time to read this chapter, I'm sure you feel the same. Encourage those who don't to open their minds and hearts to a better reality.

Enough said.

PITFALL 5: A NON-MUSICAL FOCUS

When I was in fifth grade, two uniformed police officers came to my school and proceeded to show the most horrifying film I had ever seen. The hour-long movie was real footage of heroin addicts shooting up in grungy back-alleys; emergency room workers shoving tubes up the noses of unconscious overdose patients; and screaming, sobbing, chemically-altered people whose pained ravings made no sense. I spent the majority of the hour looking at my shoes, feeling queasy, and wondering if anyone was going to barf as had happened when my sister's class had seen this notorious film. I made a mental note to avoid any activities that could lead to a cameo in a police department documentary.

Twenty years later, I am watching a jazz combo play a concert at a middle school. The ensemble is making a futile attempt to convey the same anti-drug message as the police film, but unfortunately, their music seems a bit of a non-sequitur. Moreover, the message lacks the effectiveness and authority of professional drug prevention programs. Nobody barfs.

The next day, I watch a string quartet attempt to use works by Mozart, Ravel, and Tchaikovsky to teach third-graders about the solar system. It's never quite clear what their music has to do with space, but we take a whirlwind tour of the galaxy anyway. Afterwards, I can't remember a single fact from the planetary trivia that was hurriedly recited before each excerpt, and the kids I interview don't seem to know what a cello is.

In all fairness, both of these ensembles were merely doing the job they were asked to do. The problem lies in the agenda they were handed.

Confusing, non-musical programs result when musicians and presenters try to market their ensembles to schools and communities who are requesting or demanding curricular links or specific ideological messages.

I'm all for designing programs that appeal to the needs of schools and communities, but in the rush for relevance, two crucial principles are often forgotten:

- We musicians are experts on music. It's what we know and do best.
- The experts on drug prevention, literacy, science, math, social work, and so forth specialize in those subjects; it's what they do best.

When music becomes a mere vehicle for a non-musical agenda, both the musical presentation and the message suffer. If school administrations don't expect the police officers to burst out singing polyphonic anti-drug madrigals, why do schools and arts organizations insist that musicians make their programs serve intrinsically unmusical purposes?

> *"When music becomes a mere vehicle for a non-musical agenda, both the musical presentation and the message suffer."*

Music has merit in and of itself, and any concert of value must ground itself in musical experience. When we depart from the music, we depart from what we know and do best. We cannot be expected to teach other subjects as effectively as our counterparts in those disciplines. When musical substance takes the back burner, we no longer enjoy ourselves and neither does our audience.

Realistically, though, we may have to grapple with the fact that School X won't book any program that doesn't meet State Literacy Standard 2.9. So be it. Find a way to meet that demand with musical integrity.

> **CONSIDER THIS: FITTING THE AGENDA**
>
> If you find yourself under pressure to address non-musical agendas with your concert, consider the following advice:
>
> 1. Begin with music. Real music that you want to play. Think of more pieces than you could put in any one concert.
> 2. Look at your list and ask yourself, "What are some natural connections that could be made to meet the demands of my clients? What is a theme that could have musical meaning as well as extra-musical relevance?" If possible, involve a friend who understands your client's perspective. A non-musician may see the connections more quickly and easily than you can.
> 3. Once you've found a thematic way to connect your repertoire to the client's demands, brainstorm entry points and design activities that meet the extra-musical agenda while heightening the perception of your music.

With a little creativity, you will discover ways to satisfy your client's agenda while maintaining your musical integrity.

Here's a crucial hint: you will have the most success if your extra-musical agenda provides a metaphor with clear musical manifestations. At the Hudson Valley Philharmonic one year, we created a concert that addressed the demand for a program addressing conflict resolution by exploring how composers expressed conflict and resolution in music.

It can be done. John Bertles and Carina Piaggio's ensemble, Bash the Trash, has been performing innovative concerts, residencies, and workshops that integrate science, environmentalism, story-telling, and creative writing for thirty-plus years. Who knows? Maybe you will be the one who finally creates the effective, musically illuminating, drug-prevention jazz revue.

PITFALL 6: IRRELEVANT ACTIVITIES

Sometimes, performers and presenters think of fun, cool ideas that have no apparent connection to the repertoire that is being performed. This brings us to an important principle about our presentations:

If you don't hear a musical connection, your audience won't either.

I once saw a highly engaging, entertaining orchestra concert on PBS. The conductor's brilliant presentation and interaction led to some stunning insights into sophisticated musical works.

Then, for no apparent reason, he introduced a comedic juggling troupe, which performed its humorous shtick while the orchestra performed a . . . while the orchestra performed . . . funny, I have no recollection what the orchestra actually played. Whatever the musical selection was, it became wallpaper for an amusing act that did nothing for our ears or the orchestra.

I do have a happy example of an instance where a particularly savvy performer used a seemingly irrelevant activity to elicit serious musical insights.

Midway through a New York Philharmonic School Day Concert, conductor Bobby McFerrin decided to have a "seventh-inning stretch." Just for fun, McFerrin asked the teenage audience to do "the wave" like people do at baseball games. McFerrin made the incongruous activity all the more humorous by sending the wave from the back of the hall up through the members of the orchestra.

To bring us back from Yankee Stadium to Lincoln Center, McFerrin asked the audience, "What does 'the wave' have to do with the second movement of Mendelssohn's *Italian Symphony*? Anybody? How was the music we just played like doing 'the wave'?"

After a reflective pause, audience members began to articulate connections:

"The musicians passed themes from one instrument to the other."

"The music was flowing."

"There were waves of dynamics where it'd grow loud and then get soft."

After collecting several cogent observations, McFerrin affirmed them by saying, "Good! Now listen for all those things as we play the third and fourth movements."

Thanks to McFerrin's impulse to make a connection to the music, his "seventh inning stretch" did more than refresh our bodies: it sensitized us to the "waves" in the music that followed.

PITFALL 7: LACK OF VARIETY

Sometimes, a concert's interactions are completely relevant to the music, but they all amount to essentially the same activity. When audience interactions lack variety, participation becomes a tiresome chore.

This pitfall once surfaced at an otherwise pleasant family concert performance by a husband-and-wife folk duo at a YMCA conference center. Both of them sang and performed skillfully on autoharp, guitar, harmonica, and fiddle. Their repertoire offered a nice variety of tempi, emotions, and cultural origins. Their set was organized, well paced, and thoughtfully programmed.

The couple occasionally asked the audience to chime in during a song. Three of the opportunities involved randomly making animal sounds on cue; others involved filling in lyrical blanks. While most of the audience enjoyed the first interaction (making a chicken-clucking cacophony on cue), by about the third animal-sound song, even the youngest children lost their enthusiasm for playing along. Why? The interactive strategy was one-dimensional and not particularly musical. The novelty of participation gave way to predictability and pointlessness.

> **CONSIDER THIS: BEYOND THE ANIMAL SOUNDS**
> What could the folk duo have done to create activity variety? Here are a few possible approaches that would have deepened the interactions and engaged the audience in more varied ways:
> - The audience could learn to sing the chorus of one song so that the participation would be musically grounded. The whole concert could conclude with an audience sing-along that involves everyone.
> - The audience could create and perform a rhythmic accompaniment to a song. This process could be used to highlight how one member of the duo always provided accompaniment while the other sang or played the melody.
> - The audience could do a little internal reflective work to deepen the emotional impact of some of the more serious Appalachian ballads.
> - The audience could make up an additional verse to one of the sillier animal songs.

Seek to involve your audience in diverse and meaningful ways. If you find that your concert consists of one basic activity type, go back to chapter 4 and find creative alternatives. Try to avoid using any of the activity archetypes more than once during a concert.

PITFALL 8: FAILING TO BE AUDIENCE APPROPRIATE

Let's face it; retired Teamsters may not feel like standing up and touching their toes, and kids older than eight may feel insulted if you ask them to sing "Twinkle, Twinkle, Little Star." Conversely, an unschooled listener may not find the unconventional modulations of Prokofiev's *Classical Symphony* as hilarious as a highly trained musician with perfect pitch does. Activities involving basic physical coordination skills may be too challenging for very young audiences but regarded as "babyish" by listeners who are only a few years older.

As musicians, it's hard to be experts on every audience demographic. Consequently, we sometimes give our listeners too little or too much credit. When in doubt whether an activity, topic, or explanation is appropriate, consult people from your audience's demographic. If you cannot consult prospective audience members directly, consult someone with a thorough understanding and knowledge of their tastes and abilities. Teachers, parents, children, and professors of cognitive development or educational psychology are all wonderful resources.

> *"When in doubt whether an activity, topic, or explanation is appropriate, consult people from your audience's demographic."*

When you design an interactive performance, put yourself in your audience's shoes. Would you find the interactions fun and intriguing, or would you find them embarrassing, condescending, or overwhelmingly complex?

A jazz ensemble performing a lecture performance for a high school audience fell into this pitfall. The ensemble was knowledgeable and amazing, but their highly sophisticated and theoretical explanations went way over the audience's head until a young man raised his hand and said, "I don't get what you mean by that."

After a brief exchange, the leader of the band realized that the audience did not consist primarily of jazz students, as he had presumed. He proceeded to speak without jargon and accompanied his demonstrations with metaphors that made more sense to his listeners.

Through experience, you will develop an intuitive feel for what's right for any particular audience. In performance, be sensitive to your audience's reactions, and make adjustments accordingly.

PITFALL 9: PROBLEMATIC PIECE LENGTHS

We can run into trouble when our musical selections are too long or too short. Plan your musical selections the same way you would plan any other concert or recital. Think about pacing, style, and the overall shape. If you were to remove all the interactions and have nothing but the music, would your chosen repertoire make a good album or recital program?

Leonard Bernstein's televised *Young People's Concerts* arguably provide some of the finest examples of intelligent programming. Bernstein had an uncanny sense for ordering his selections and choosing works of an appropriate length. Consequently, each *Young People's Concert* feels like a satisfying musical experience as well as an enlightening educational event. Moreover, Bernstein also set the repertoire bar high by programming challenging contemporary works alongside timeless classics. Bernstein never "dumbed down."

So, what is too long or too short?

It's difficult to establish hard-and-fast rules, but based on experience and Bernstein's example, in an orchestral situation, eight minutes seems to be a reasonable limit for what a young or inexperienced audience can comfortably digest. At the other end of the spectrum, too many instrumental selections under three minutes can feel like watching an endless stream of television commercials. Create a balance between longer works and shorter ones. When performing longer selections, it can help to let the audience know the approximate duration.

Sometimes in planning concerts, performers must confront the issue of making cuts—leaving out some of the piece in order to reduce its length. Some musicians maintain a deep philosophical aversion to making any cuts. That's fine; just be aware that longer durations place more demands on your audience's attention, so choose your repertoire accordingly. On occasion, I have lost the attention of some audience members by programming works that were too long for them. Once their focus had lapsed, it was very hard to regain it.

Bernstein did make cuts, and once again, he sets a superlative example. Most of the time, unless you have a score in front of you, you will not even realize that he has made a cut. If you do make cuts, strive to make them as unobtrusive as possible.

PITFALL 10: DISENGAGED PERFORMERS

We've all seen it. A dynamic group leader is doing an outstanding job of communicating the joy of music and engaging her audience while the rest of the group is slouching, looking bored, or projecting an attitude of inattention and disinterest. More often than not, this disengaged appearance is the result of shyness, inexperience, or obliviousness, rather than belligerence.

To rectify this situation, the leader should use her dynamic communication skills to draw out the more reticent performers. I'm a firm believer in actively involving every member of a band or small chamber ensemble at least once during a concert. Even if a performer is not comfortable speaking, he can participate when the audience is participating or help lead activities nonverbally. Often, the very act of joining in for one activity will keep a performer more interested throughout the rest of the event.

With large ensembles, look for ways to involve the entire ensemble in a large-group activity, and ask willing volunteers to come forward to lead various parts of the presentation.

If you still find yourself in a group of chronic slouchers, please stress to them—better yet, have an objective observer of your dress rehearsal stress to them—how important it is to look alert, smile, make eye contact with the audience, participate in activities, and remain visibly focused on whatever is happening at the moment. Better still, video a rehearsal, and let people see their demeanors for themselves.

Don't settle for apathy. Inaction speaks louder than words.

CHAPTER 7

Deeper Audience Engagement

Performing arts organizations everywhere are working to increase the depth and scope of their community and audience engagement. Isolated "one-shot" outreach events are gradually being replaced by residencies, series, and online engagement strategies. Today's artists are developing programs that offer multiple artistic encounters that are accompanied by preparation, creative participation, and follow-up.

One of the primary reasons behind this dramatic shift is the realization that most people cannot become lifelong participants and supporters of the arts through random, isolated experiences. However, if artistic encounters happen within the context of ongoing immersion in the arts, they have a more substantial and meaningful impact.

Similarly, a healthy fan base thrives on connection and continued engagement. As interactive performers, we should strive to maximize the impact of our work by deepening our approach. On the most basic level, we can extend the reach of our performances by preceding and following each concert with a related event or workshop.

> *"As interactive performers, we should strive to maximize the impact of our work by deepening our approach."*

PRECONCERT WORKSHOPS, TALKS, AND EVENTS

Preconcert events have long been a musical staple. Growing up, I remember how local pop, rock, and country radio stations would give away tickets to pre-show festivities where a lucky few people would meet major artists and go to the concert. Because the events were broadcast, the rest of us would get a bit of a window into the musicians, life on the road, and their music. Similarly, cultural centers often engage their artists in preconcert talks.

If you are being interviewed, have a few sound bites ready. Build in a few teasers about your performance. Share a few details or secrets about the music you're going to play. Build some anticipation and suspense. If at all possible, play or sing. Music often proves more powerful than words at these events.

If you are hired as a lecturer or host who interviews an artist, strive to make the event interactive. If your listeners learn a specific rhythm, or a chorus, or sing a portion of the music, they will engage with active rather than passive understanding.

Artists now use more hands-on, audience-centered approaches that give people a more active role. The Cooperstown Chamber Music Festival precedes its family concerts with workshops based on the concert theme. They follow their performances with an "instrument petting zoo" where the performers help audience members try out instruments. [5]

---

5. Linda Chesis, artistic director and flutist, reports that students have returned in subsequent years to report that they now take lessons on an instrument they had tried out the year before.

FIG. 7.1. Preconcert Activities at the Cooperstown Chamber Music Festival. Photo courtesy of Linda Chesis.

At one of the festival's family concerts featuring Copland's complete *Appalachian Spring* for thirteen instruments, the musicians offered a one-hour, multi-station preparatory workshop. The walls were covered with mural paper and the audience was invited to add their own drawings to create a panoramic picture of the rural American landscape. Folk dancers taught people dance steps for the Shaker melody "Simple Gifts," as a violinist from the ensemble performed it. At another station, the concertgoers made "musical quilts" by gluing leather musical notes, fabric, and symbols to muslin sheets. Once a quilt was finished, it could be taken to a musician who would perform the notes. After the concert, children took their quilt squares home as souvenirs.

The musicians also held a "musical Olympics" where they competed to see who could play the loudest, the fastest, the softest, and so forth. All the events of the preconcert workshop served either to highlight the contextual mood of Copland's work or to introduce the instruments and the themes they would play. Consequently, the audience was able to focus for the entire uninterrupted performance of the work.

The preconcert workshop approach works for adults as well. In a program entitled *Samba vs. Tango: The Cultural Contrasts of South America*,[6] Chris Perry and Erin Furbee of the Oregon Symphony put together an incredible six-station preconcert workshop. Ticket-buyers could learn to tango, go to samba school, try out Latin percussion instruments, watch a slide show of Carnival images, try on Carnival costumes, and meet a strolling bandoneon player who demonstrated his instrument and answered questions. To ensure attendance of the preconcert event, tickets announced the starting time as 7:00 P.M. (the time of the workshop), although the performance itself began at 8:00 P.M. Given the fun nature of the activities—and the free, thematic food and drinks—patrons responded with delight at the unanticipated surprise.

As enjoyable as the preconcert activities were, they were not just games and light entertainment. Most of them cleverly familiarized listeners with the rhythms, timbres, instruments, and genres they would hear during the concert. The workshop was a preparation as much as it was a party.

> **CONSIDER THIS: IDEAS FOR PRE-CONCERT AND POST-CONCERT ACTIVITIES**
>
> With a little planning, you can create fun events and workshops to precede or follow your concerts. Here is a brief list of offerings, which have proven enjoyable for a wide range of audiences:
>
> - Stations for trying real instruments or building homemade ones.
> - Mini-performances by musicians, actors, dancers, or storytellers.
> - Opportunities to interact with musicians and composers.
> - Music or dance lessons.
> - Workshops that prepare the audience for an opportunity to perform in the concert.
> - Workshops where people compose something to be performed during the concert.
> - Food and drink.
> - Interviews or a broadcast "Meet the Artist" event.
> - Mementos or "gift bags," which can be taken home. Be sure to include a bumper sticker or other appropriate items promoting your ensemble.

---

6. For a complete description of this program, see Eric Booth's Article "Edifications: Fuller Audience Engagement: Sure, but What Does It Look Like?" *Chamber Music* Vol. 20 no. 3 (June 2003): 22–23. *Chamber Music* is a great resource for interactive concert ideas.

CONCERT SERIES

As phenomenal as a single event may be, for long-term impact, the audience needs repeated musical experiences. Try creating a series of at least three interactive concerts. For maximum effect, have each build or expand on the material of the preceding concert. Create annually recurring events and find ways to promote them.

Also start thinking about ways of reaching your audiences before the day of the event. When partnering with schools and other organizations, you can deepen the concert experience by offering preparatory workshops and literature in the days preceding the performance.

With Young Audiences and many performing arts organizations, classroom teachers generally receive a study guide of preparatory activities, as well as recorded excerpts of the concert repertoire. (Helpful hint: the guides and recordings are most likely to be used if they are sent to the music teachers.) To help teachers use the study guide most effectively, teaching artists offer teachers' workshops where they lead teachers through the activities step by step.

After the classroom teacher has prepared the students, a teaching artist or an ensemble visits the school and leads a workshop and performance for students. Having been thoroughly prepared, students attend the fully interactive orchestra concert. Following the event, teachers and teaching artists can help students reflect on the event by leading follow-up activities from the teachers' guide.

> **CONSIDER THIS: OVERALL ENGAGEMENT STRATEGY**
>
> Develop an overall audience engagement strategy for yourself or your ensembles. As you develop your repertoire and your programs, develop workshops, marketing materials, and educational materials. Develop online resources for teachers and presenters on your website. Interactive performance and community engagement require a substantial investment of work and time; aim to develop material and programs that you can do more than once.
>
> Create a dedicated EPK (electronic press kit) for targeting the educational and community engagement markets. Generate video content of your best work. Once you have some solid successes, develop a marketing and promotional strategy. Groups and artists that develop strong audience engagement abilities, a vital online presence, and a strong track record for meaningful work get noticed.

SHORT-TERM RESIDENCY

For an even deeper approach, you can develop a short-term, intensive residency at one location. Andrew Appel, of the baroque chamber group the Four Nations Ensemble, has developed a highly successful week-long model for working in public schools.

FIG. 7.2. The Four Nations Ensemble in Residence in the South Bronx. Photo credit: David Rodgers.

Every morning, the Four Nations Ensemble performs a concert for the entire school. During the day, the ensemble members visit individual classrooms where they lead hands-on workshops. The students practice listening skills, discuss what they hear, share their interpretations with one another, and draw pictures inspired by music.

One ingenious aspect of the Four Nations Ensemble's approach is their strategy for developing attention spans. The first assembly performance is brief and introductory. With each following day, the duration of the morning performance is incrementally increased. By the end of the week, the students are ready to focus for a full 45-minute musical performance.

On the last day, students, teachers, and principals express how much they wish the ensemble could become a permanent part of the school. The residency culminates in a Saturday concert with the local orchestra, which buses the students and their parents to the concert hall.

LONG-TERM PARTNERSHIPS AND RESIDENCIES

The most intensive outreach programs entail long-term partnerships and residencies. While we often look to larger arts organizations to provide communities with such programs, individual musicians and groups are capable of designing long-term residencies as well. The Ying Quartet has achieved wide acclaim for its incredibly in-depth, multi-year community residencies sponsored by the National Endowment for the Arts, Chamber Music America, and other organizations.

When the Yings are in residence, they work hard to reach every part of the community. In addition to their evening concert series, the group gives workshops and performances in every conceivable venue: churches, hospitals, schools, businesses, homes, social clubs, and more. By the end of the residency, the entire community embraces the quartet and its music. The experience is rewarding for the quartet as well, and they make a point of returning to perform in the years following the residency.

In a similar vein, Flobots, an alternative rock/hip-hop group, has engaged its community on a local level in Colorado. With educational workshops, voter registration drives, political rallies, protests, and social justice campaigns, the group pushes to educate, motivate, and inspire action.

Of course, they are following in the footsteps of many other artists, and bands use their music as an opportunity for social engagement on a community and national level. Study the lives and words of musicians like Marian Anderson, Pete Seeger, Chuck D, Joan Baez, and others who use(d) their music to build community, engage community, and effect change.

If you want to have the same kind of impact in your hometown, begin strategizing a community outreach plan today. Define your purpose as a musician, ensemble, or organization, and determine whom you most desire to target in your community. It is better to do a thorough, in-depth job of reaching a smaller segment of the population than to try to reach all of the people in a limited, scattershot fashion.

Once you have a plan, seek sponsors and apply for grants with local, state, and national arts councils. There is a significant amount of available aid, but it must be pursued. If you can hire a professional grant writer or development director, you will likely save yourself time while receiving more funding than you might discover on your own. Many grant writers will work on a per-hour or per-project basis.

In addition to assistance with the financial part of outreach, professional development for concert design and presentation is gradually becoming available. As musicians become more and more skilled in this work, growing numbers of mentors and consultants are available to help others. ASCAP, BMI, Chamber Music America, the League of American Orchestras, and various arts-in-education organizations provide workshops, seminars, and forums for improving our presentational, planning, and marketing skills.

FOLLOWING UP: ENGAGING VIRTUALLY

Because we live in a world of twenty-four-hour connectedness, you have the ability to continue connecting and building community outside of your performance. Keep an active online presence. Precede and follow your events with strategic social media campaigns that continue to build your presence, community, and dialogue with your fans. Share photos and videos of concert highlights, and keep your fans' interest kindled.

In-depth approaches clearly require considerable planning and vision, but the dividends are well worth the investment. In time, we can build enduring relationships in our community and foster a lifelong love of music in our audiences. And if we accomplish that, our art will always have a future.

PART III

Reaching Out in the Real World

CHAPTER 8

Engagement Everywhere: Performing in Schools, Hospitals, Prisons, Comedy Clubs, and More

A mindset of engagement broadens your perspective on performing. Any space is a potential venue; any group of people is a prospective audience. That said, each context might require unique adjustments for engaging your listeners effectively and navigating the social parameters successfully.

Before we explore common interactive performance scenarios, let's reinforce some universal precepts for staying on course and finding the right tone:

1. **People are people.** To quote Depeche Mode's Martin Gore, "People are people." You are not performing for prisoners, parishioners, preschoolers, geriatric patients, millennials, metal-heads, "bluebloods," or any other limiting stereotype.

    The instant you label an audience, you "other" it. You erect psychological barriers by substituting your assumptions for your audience's human potential.

    People perceive. *People* interpret. *People* feel and respond. If you regard your listeners as human beings, you'll tap the empathetic power of your music. You won't judge, condescend, or ignore. Remember that all of us have the power to enjoy music and to participate in something greater than ourselves.

2. **Focus on sharing.** At each performance, you and your listeners share time and art. Each event is a precious communal experience, never to be exactly repeated.

What do you have to say as an artist today? What do you long to give this particular audience? What gift might you receive in return? When I ask myself these questions, everything from repertoire, to message, to pacing and emotional trajectory falls into place.

3. **Focus on gratitude.** Never forget how blessed you are to have musical gifts, wonderful colleagues, a gig, an audience, or a performance space. Yes, you may have a 5 A.M. call time, too little warm-up, inadequate lighting or acoustics, hecklers, or colleagues who aren't into it.

   However, when you have the stage and the microphone, you're in control. If you remain calm, collected, and grateful, your audience will quickly come to reflect your example. Greet everyone with, "I'm glad to see you!" or "We're thrilled to be with you tonight!" Mean it.

4. **Know the scene.** Most performance situations and venues have set parameters. Do your homework. Know the scene. Visit the venue and observe a typical performance, if you can. Get to know musicians who are already working a particular circuit and ask their advice. Know the personnel who are helping to organize the event, and be sure that you have their contact information.

   Some venues may require you to bring your own music stands, amplifiers, or other equipment. You may need to make special arrangements for parking, load-in, or security clearance. Allow for extra setup time. As my electric guitarist Dana Scofidio is fond of saying, "An hour early is on time." Have you ever in your life regretted being early?

5. **Know the audience.** Try to find out as much as you can about your audiences in advance of your performances. What is their personal background, age, typical life experience? What is their motivation for coming to a particular performance? Your presenters and hosts can usually tell you a great deal about your listeners. The better you know your audience, the better you can program your concert to connect. Assume nothing. When in doubt, ask questions—of both your presenters and of your audiences.

6. **Be a good and gracious guest.** At any venue, consider yourself to be a guest in someone else's home. Abide by your host's rules of operation and codes of conduct. Respect everyone present. Remember to send a thank you note or gift to people who helped you.
7. **Build partnerships and community.** Look at each performance as an opportunity to build a lasting relationship with a specific presenter, venue, and audience. A musical career entails building long-term relationships and creating and participating in a community. When you visit unique venues, you have a chance to add another community and additional audience members to your own. Look to book a repeat performance; consider what you may bring your listeners the next time.
8. **Be yourself.** Regardless of your audience or your venue, you'll be most successful and most comfortable if you simply be yourself and do what you do best. Some venues or circumstances may require you to set aside aspects of your life, your story, or your art temporarily (I'm thinking of a colleague who consciously has to curb his onstage profanity for some audiences), but you should still seek to be authentically yourself.

SCHOOLS

Educational concerts provide an important cultural role in the life of most schoolchildren. Substantial performance and residency opportunities exist through Young Audiences, arts councils, and other cultural organizations.

Be in touch with the school's classroom teachers and music specialists before and after your event. Ask if there are ways you can help support their work. Having preparatory and follow-up materials for the classroom teachers can also increase the potential impact of your concert. A good relationship with teachers can lead to better preparation and follow-up with students. Moreover, sometimes teachers weigh in on a school's arts programming.

Some schools have ideal, state-of-the-art auditoriums; others are more outdated. In either setting, you will likely need some help with lighting, setting up a P.A. system, or just getting enough chairs. Custodians are some of the most essential members of the school community. Often, they are the ones who will come to your rescue when you need someone to unlock the piano, access the stage lights, or set up a P.A. system.

Schools are one of the most inviting environments for a fully interactive show. All of the strategies and advice from the preceding chapters apply. Be adventurous, and if possible, document your work so that you can learn from it. Some schools have media consent forms that establish parental permission for any photos and video that are taken or published throughout the year. If you are planning on filming video for public posting, be sure that you've gotten consent.

HOSPITALS

Most patients' hospital experiences entail a considerable degree of worry, pain, exhaustion, frustration, or boredom. Live music can go a long way towards alleviating stress and establishing a healthy atmosphere for patients and family. Hospitals really could use your music.

For a number of years, I regularly played hospital concerts with violist Stephanie Griffin, my partner in the Wallgriff Duo. We did everything: lobby concerts, concerts for visiting family members, performances at nurses' central stations, visits to AIDS wards, shows in the playrooms of children's cancer wards, addiction recovery clinics, outpatient facilities, and more. Here are some of the lessons we learned.

Because many people's nerves may be on edge, or they may be grappling with emotionally complex situations, music that is beautiful, consonant, major mode, calming, uplifting, or slightly upbeat tends to garner the most appreciation. While classical music does well, recognizable popular songs, hymns, folk tunes, jazz pieces, and original compositions also have a place.

If you are performing for young children, prepare for requests. Know your nursery rhyme tunes; know songs from the currently popular kiddie films and cartoons. Purchase or create arrangements. Include sing-along songs, and be able to teach them to listeners who do not know them. If parents are present, encourage them to participate alongside their children.

Sometimes, a hospital may position you where you do not have a set audience. (For example, I've often been stationed in a hallway or a nurses' station where the music can fill the entire wing, but there are no seats near me.) In these situations, focus on creating a continuous flow of music, and segue from one piece to the next naturally.

When you do have an audience, remember to communicate. Listening to patients can be just as important as playing for them. Be aware that some patients—especially those with serious pain or late-stage terminal illnesses—may not feel like participating actively. Before you play anything, try to find out a bit more about the people in your audience. If you can, find out what music they enjoy or find calming or energizing. You want to play the repertoire that for them carries hope, optimism, or positive associations. At any particular session, be sensitive to people's moods, feelings, and preferred means of enjoying the music. Be prepared to change repertoire, or even to stop, if what you are playing doesn't seem to help.

In the patients' (and your own) best interests, you should be healthy, appropriately dressed, and compliant with sanitary procedures before and after your visit.

> **CONSIDER THIS: MUSIC AND WELLNESS**
>
> Pittsburgh Symphony musician Penny Brill helped her orchestra to create a Music and Wellness program, which has enjoyed many years of success. Penny had rediscovered the therapeutic power of music following her own personal battle against breast cancer, which had included chemotherapy and five surgeries. Once she recovered, Penny started to make clinical visits and began to advocate.
>
> As the Music and Wellness program developed, it expanded to include more of Penny's colleagues, the Music Therapy Department at Duquesne University, the University of Pittsburgh Medical Center's hospitals, the Veterans Affairs Pittsburgh Health Care system, and other local, national, and international partners.
>
> Central to the program's success, the Music and Wellness program pairs world-class musicians with resident music therapists who work together in meeting patients' needs and goals. Goals may range from clinically measurable results such as reduced blood pressure to psychological goals (e.g., patients having less depression or a greater sense of control and a more active role in treatment). Programs are coordinated to accomplish the patients' goals, and the music serves to engage, relax, or energize listeners.
>
> The Pittsburgh Symphony created a website (http://wellness.pittsburghsymphony.org) to serve as a resource and information hub for musicians and organizations who seek to establish and develop music and wellness programs. You will find a handbook for developing and implementing your own programs, as well as links to many relevant resources and organizations.

PSYCHIATRIC FACILITIES

Ancient Greek philosopher Plato wrote extensively about music's power to influence mood and behavior. Today, a holistic approach to psychiatric care commonly includes music therapy or musical instruction. In mental health contexts, your performances can provide healing, empathy, focus, and an emotional outlet.

Concerts at psychiatric facilities can run a wide gamut. I've performed concerts for quiet, sedate patients, as well as rollicking events that spontaneously became joyful dance parties. Many shows designed for school or community centers can be easily adapted for psychiatric facilities.

If possible, work with a facility, its doctors, nurses, and clinicians to create concerts that fit into a larger therapeutic plan. Composer Richard Carrick and I once designed a concert at New York's Bellevue Hospital, in coordination with program directors of its World Trade Center Environmental Health Center. Participants included patients receiving ongoing treatment for traumas, depression, and various physical, mental, and emotional disorders related to the September 11th terrorist attacks.

The concert took place on the eleventh anniversary of the attacks. The lobby atrium where we performed also doubled as an art gallery filled with paintings created by patients during art therapy sessions. Some depicted burning buildings; others projected emotions via abstract shapes. Most poignantly, many pictures featured angels amidst the chaos.

Our concert served as a motivation for people to get out of their houses, and hopefully, to take their minds to a better place. Immediately following the concert, some listeners had additional therapy sessions.

Of all the interactive performances Rick and I had scripted over the years, this was arguably one of the simplest to put together. As New Yorkers, our level of empathy and identification with the patients was extraordinarily high. We needed the therapeutic impact of the music, too.

Rick and I decided that our concert would not directly address the attacks or the anniversary. Instead, we focused on music that would reinforce a sense of calm, peace, faith, safety, and beauty. In consultation with the unit's doctors, we put together a program of classical works, several of our own compositions, traditional fiddling, and gospel hymns. Throughout, we spoke in third person point-of-view to set an inclusive, unifying tone and establish group rapport.

As we performed in Bellevue's lobby, the sound of our instruments echoed throughout the hospital. Many doctors stopped to listen, or people came by to eat their lunches, or to visit paintings in the gallery. By the end of the event, almost everyone I encountered was smiling, and had a relaxed, rested demeanor. On a personal level, I felt more peace than I ever had on a September 11th anniversary. I renewed my resolve to use music to fight anxieties, depression, and fear.

Admittedly, sometimes establishing a calm, therapeutic atmosphere and environment can be difficult. Once, I arrived at a psychiatric ward at a hospital on Long Island to perform *Improvisational Journey*. (See page 141.) As the door locked behind me, I surveyed a packed common room as I slowly unpacked my instruments. A silent man with a vacuous stare drooled out of the side of his mouth. A woman in a wheelchair occasionally spontaneously screamed. Another man furiously and continuously muttered at himself under his breath, while another repeatedly sang the first line of "On Top of Old Smokey."

I paused. The atmosphere was not hostile, but it was diffuse, disturbed, and disordered. While a few orderlies were present, my contact had left me to fend for myself; there would be no formal welcome or introduction. If I wanted calm, focus, and order, I would need to establish it.

Because I didn't think that speaking or clapping for attention would help, I softly began playing the "Prelude" from Bach's C major cello suite and hoped for the best. To my wonderment, the chaos gradually dissipated, and the room settled into quiet. Something about the harmonies and arpeggios seemed to soothe people's spirits and establish mental order. By the end of the movement, I had everyone's attention and was able to continue as planned.

In psychiatric facilities, as in all situations, be prepared to adjust and change course, if necessary. Remember to trust that your music has a power of its own.

CORRECTIONAL FACILITIES

Country star Johnny Cash arguably set the gold standard for audience engagement behind bars. His uncut recordings *At Folsom Prison* and *At San Quentin* reveal a band connecting, amusing, moving, and uplifting its audience from first downbeat to final encore.

Undoubtedly, Cash's own experiences running afoul of the law and serving time added credence and a unique ability to identify authentically with his audience. However, consider an observation from Merle Haggard, an eventual country music star who was an inmate during Cash's first San Quentin State Prison performance: ". . . nobody except me and about fifteen guys cared for the fact that he was coming because country music was at an all-time low. Most everybody listened to rock & roll, blues, jazz whatever." According to Haggard, by the end of the evening, everyone was a fan.

How did Cash connect with his literally captive audience who normally would neither have enjoyed nor responded to his milieu?

Track down the videos and records of these performances, and have a listen. Enjoy the shows, and take notes. Cash treats his audience with respect and addresses the men as his peers, his equals. He chooses songs exploring universal narratives of love, loss, suffering, redemption, humor, and faith. He shares new material for the first time, including songs written for that night's audience. He shares stories, asks rhetorical questions, converses. Throughout, Cash leads the crowd's energy with his strength, assurance, and genuine understanding.

By the time these concerts were recorded, Johnny Cash had performed multiple times at both prisons, so he had built a rapport and a sense of community. He came with nothing to prove. He simply served, entertained, and loved his listeners—with winking humor, protest songs, story songs, ballads, or hymns.

Needless to say, there was only one Johnny Cash. We may not have served time. We may not exude fashion, fame, or inherent "cool," and our music may not even have lyrics. Still, if we are comfortable being ourselves and sharing our music with skill, sincerity, and respect, we can make the same humane connections and provide similar encounters with beauty and truth.

I had the privilege of working with electric violinist, singer, and composer Tracy Silverman as he prepared his first ever correctional facility visit and performance. Tracy's concert would take place in an adult women's detention center near Burlington, Vermont, as part of his residency with the Community Engagement Lab (CEL). [7]

---

7. The Community Engagement Lab, founded by conductor Paul Gambill and teaching artist Eric Booth, initially began as a nonprofit consortium that commissioned composers and performing artists to create thematic new works while simultaneously designing community engagement residencies for the composer, artist, and teaching artists. www.communityengagementlab.org

Preparing this solo show on relatively short notice, Tracy had plenty of questions, ranging from logistics to philosophical questions regarding his role. As someone who was neither a woman nor an ex-offender, Tracy naturally wondered what to say and not say. He had no desire to preach, condescend, or to make light of serious realities.

Dennis Bonanza, our liaison with the facility, provided some helpful perspective: "Look, it's voluntary. Anyone there will be glad to see you. It'll be the best part of their day. Just do what you do." He did request a few songs that he enjoyed and believed would break the ice and connect well with the inmates. [8]

Combining pop music, country music, hard rock instrumentals, Bach, and complex original compositions involving a Boomerang Phrase Sampler looper, Tracy took Dennis's advice and delivered a performance of much of the same material he had played at his community theater show a few days prior.

The primary difference? In addition to learning Dennis's song requests, and developing his own version of Beth Nielsen Chapman's "Heads Up for the Wrecking Ball," Tracy tweaked his underlying theme and spoken narrative to focus on his own personal journey of finding his voice as a musician and accepting himself.

In contrast to Cash, Tracy made no overt acknowledgement of the inmates' circumstances, and generally treated his audience just like any other. He encouraged them to clap and sing, and gave inquisitive listeners a chance to operate his wah pedal. His approach remained fully participatory, and the women fully participated.

The concert had many great moments, but the emotional highpoint was Tracy's jazzy reinterpretation of a "Largo" by J.S. Bach. While his performance was expressive and stunning in its own right, it followed closely on the heels of a poignant autobiographical story.

---

8. Note: When preparing an event in a correctional facility, remember to consider staff's opinions, suggestions, and requests. They usually know the people and the environment better than we do, and they are also valued audience members.

Tracy detailed his own personal struggles to fit into rigid and prohibitive musical establishments and highly standardized repertoire. Tracy concluded, "I finally realized that I couldn't change these things; the only thing I could change was myself." The process of accepting himself and developing his authentic voice ultimately gave him permission to freely express himself on his own terms.

Like Johnny Cash, Tracy's Bach presentation had delivered a palpable lesson without being pedantic. It came honestly from his own life experience. He gave us the hope that we also might surmount life's challenges to embody our full potential and beauty. Because Tracy made himself vulnerable, we listeners were, too. As I looked around, I saw more than a few tears.

Logistics

For many correctional facilities, you will need to undergo a background check in advance. (The facility or your presenting organization can help you with that.) When you visit, bring a government ID, and allow considerable extra time for going through security and storing any disallowed items in a locker. You will need to know and respect the rules and conventions of the facility, which may include specific details related to dress, language, communication, contact, and any procedures related to your visit.

As an interactive performer, you will want to make sure that any participatory parts of your show comply with any restrictions, or are appropriately adjusted. Do include participatory elements when possible, as they really do connect.

While a single performance can be a wonderful experience, you will have a deeper and more transformative impact if you become a part of the community, perform regularly, or commit to longer residencies that provide inmates with musical training and performance opportunities.

HOUSES OF WORSHIP AND RELIGIOUS COMMUNITIES

Considerably many performance opportunities exist within religious communities, or are hosted in their facilities. Musicians can enjoy a broad range of roles ranging from performing secular programs in sacred spaces to leading worship and teaching via music.

Communities of faith usually have strong networks. More often than not, one successful event can lead to many more. Word of mouth is strong, so let's be mindful of the subtleties that can help to establish connections and build long-term relationships.

Whether or not we subscribe to any faith, when we perform in a religious venue or context, we are entering somebody's sacred space. More than ever, we need to be mindful of being a respectful guest.

When I perform in a synagogue with klezmer musician Yale Strom's Broken Consort, I wear a yarmulke, if it's clear that most of the men hosting or attending do. In Catholic churches, I make sure that I'm not inadvertently using their altar as my prop table. During a residency at Osaka's Soai University (a Buddhist school), I made sure to know whether or not shoes were allowed in my various performance and workshop spaces.

Let your dress, language, and conduct respect your hosts and audiences at all times, whether or not you agree with their faith, theology, or public stances as a community. While I've occasionally seen performers seize religious contexts as opportunities to push the envelope of appropriateness, make personal political statements, or even chide their listeners, I've never seen it effect change or make a constructive impact.

At the same time, spiritual communities do seek musicians and teaching artists who can engage them on challenging questions, philosophical questions, and matters of faith. You can design workshops, residencies, and performances that explore specific spiritual themes and questions. The key is to choose repertoire and activities that lead participants to think, discover, and find their own applications.

One of my longtime friends, Reverend James Hodsden, is a Presbyterian pastor whose congregations have hired me to serve as a guest artist for multi-day, topically focused spiritual enrichment retreats led by a guest speaker.

I correspond and converse with James and the speaker far in advance so that my workshops, interstitial performances, and culminating interactive concerts explore and amplify specific questions and teachings.

One year, the retreat focused on the first question of the Heidelberg Catechism: *What is your only comfort in life and in death?* The Heidelberg Catechism was new to me, but as I reflected on the question and its prescribed answer, each line suggested repertoire related to its implications. The catechism's words became entry points into music, which in turn illuminated the message.

My culminating concert became something of a liturgical service. Between communal recitations of lines from the catechism, I built in interactive and reflective segments that expounded and musically illustrated each theological point.

Afterwards, Rev. Hodsden reflected, "At our spiritual enrichment retreat, we were trying to convey some pretty profound and abstract ideas. Your musical selections and explorations helped people to understand the catechism's text at an accessible, yet much deeper level. The music provided more than an aesthetic experience. Rather, you brought profound theological concepts to life in ways that allowed people to receive and understand them."

> **CONSIDER THIS: GIGS LEAD TO GIGS**
>
> When you get booked to play a concert hosted by a congregation or community of faith, it potentially can open the doors to additional concerts. Even if you are simply a section player or a side person, get to know the community, its musical tastes, the people in charge, their affiliates.
>
> When I lived in New York City, I inadvertently stumbled into the Episcopal Church circuit. Initially, I was hired to play in orchestras for oratorios at an Upper East Side church. Within a few years, those gigs multiplied as my name remained on the list of organists and directors of music, who in turn would refer me to other directors of music. Along the way, I met good musicians who sometimes needed a violist or violinist.
>
> Before long, the oratorio work led to me being asked to perform chamber music concerts at the churches. Opportunities to help contract and curate series arose. Some series specifically wished to include non-classical bookings, which opened the door to my Texas fiddling trio playing outdoor events and concerts.
>
> Most of the opportunities came directly from having done a good job of interacting with a congregation and building a relationship with the people in charge. In hindsight, most of the opportunities unfolded naturally and without a conscious effort to pursue these kinds of bookings. Had I been strategic and active about promotion, my ensembles and I could have enjoyed even more concerts and opportunities.
>
> If you wish to pursue faith-based performance opportunities, make it a visible part of your web presence and your press kit. Make people aware of the services you can offer, keep your contacts fresh, and be sure that you always have a booking or two on your calendar.

COMEDY CLUBS

Music has been a part of comedy for centuries. In fact, until the second half of the twentieth century, comics rarely gave full-length solo performances. Stand-up comedy existed as one part of variety shows and vaudeville, both of which included a good dose of live music. With today's established venues and market for comedy, engaging musicians have an opportunity to renew our relationship with comedy and drama.

Several years into my interactive performance journey, comedienne Donna East asked me to provide musical entertainment for a clean comedy showcase. She was curating a weekly *Casual Comedy Night* at the Lamb's Theatre near Times Square. At the midpoint of the evening, I would perform an approximately seven-minute segment as an interlude between the opening amateur acts and a headlining professional comic.

The opportunity was intriguing, but I'll be honest: I had never been a huge fan of stand-up comedy. Rather, I grew up appreciating the anti-comedy of Steve Martin and Andy Kaufman, the comedic storytelling and character acting of Whoopi Goldberg and Eddie Murphy, and the absurdist irony of Jerry Seinfeld and Steven Wright. Unlike some musicians, I don't have a gift for conventional joke-telling.

Trying to be funny can backfire or feel awkward. Rather than attempt to be a bona fide comedian, I focused on my musical gifts.

I also embraced my function: my job was to reengage the audience after the amateur sets, and to build the energy and hype for the final act. If I made the audience laugh, great. If I didn't, at least they enjoyed some good music, and the headlining comic would seem all the funnier.

Along the way, though, I discovered my own comfort and voice in comedic settings. Musical entry points served as source material for fun, audience participation, and incidental humor.

Over my stand-up tenure, I developed a number of formulas and techniques that worked for me. Sometimes, I performed a new, comedic song created just for that occasion. Other times, I improvised or composed something new on the spot, based on audience suggestions or participation. Stories, anecdotes, and obscure details from my life as a musician often proved amusing or intriguing for listeners. (As a musician, you do have a somewhat unusual existence. Don't take it for granted.) I was surprised to see how quickly the audience embraced me and whatever music I shared, even if it was dissonant or avant-garde.

I scripted a few skits involving others, and sometimes became a character. If other actors or comics needed a straight man or a musical accompaniment, I was happy to oblige. My favorite moments involved getting the audience to create music together. Nothing beats filling a small room with an audience's spontaneous, joyous, live music.

I hope that you will spend some time observing and performing in comedy venues. You will learn vast amounts from observing actors' and comedians' stage presence, audience engagement, delivery, and timing. You will also gain invaluable experience from the instantaneous feedback, applause, and dialogue that happens on the comedy stage. These lessons will pay dividends for any performance or interpersonal situation.

BARS, CAFÉS, COFFEE HOUSES, AND NIGHTCLUBS

Of course, music also goes hand in hand with food, drink, and entertainment. Many musicians and bands first learned to hone their public performance skills in restaurants, bars, and clubs. At some venues (e.g., very noisy bars without stages, or elite country clubs and five-star restaurants), your music creates ambience, and you are not expected to interact directly with the patrons. However, for many venues, music is the primary attraction, and you have much more freedom—and imperative—to engage your audience. Many of the strategies and approaches we've discussed in this book will apply.

For a few years, I was part of *Music Unlocked!*, a collective of teaching artist musicians and composers who enjoyed a residency at the 92nd Street Y. One of their performance venues, 92Y Tribeca, hosts a stage, a bar, and a restaurant. We designed a number of interactive chamber music and new music concerts aimed at engaging a knowledgeable, adult audience.

Before the event, members of our ensemble went into the audience, greeting and getting to know the guests, in addition to laying the groundwork for the performance. Sometimes, we had them compose motives that would later be used in improvisations. Other times, we engaged them in a conversation that they would later realize related to the context of a particular piece on the program.

With each program, we devised a different way to engage the pre-show audience so that a degree of unpredictability would keep return patrons guessing. Because we knew we were playing for a music-loving audience, we kept the in-concert interactions more concentrated and condensed.

Before you play a club, café, or restaurant, get to know the scene, the personnel, the typical patrons, and the acts that typically play there. Notice how the performers engage the audience, and think of ways you might go a step or two beyond what is expected so that your own music stands out and connects.

Sarah Robinson's book *Clubbing for Classical Musicians* provides additional tips for performing for adults in the club scene, as well as building partnerships and bookings with the venues.

BUSKING

Some years ago, a renowned *Washington Post* journalist enlisted a Grammy-winning instrumentalist in an experiment. The artist would play publicly in an arcade just outside of a Washington D.C. Metro station. The purpose? To conduct "an experiment in context, perception, and priorities—as well as an unblinking assessment of public taste: In a banal setting at an inconvenient time, would beauty transcend?" [9]

When all was said and done, after forty-three minutes, the artist—whose professional fees can average over $1,000 a minute—grossed $32.17 in revenue from unwitting strangers. The author won a Pulitzer prize for his resulting article, which implied that in mundane settings, the general public will neither recognize nor appreciate great art or great artists.

After reading the article and watching the time-lapse video of the busking experiment, something didn't feel right. I once had earned considerably more money in less than five minutes of spontaneous busking (first movement of Mozart's *Eine kleine Nachtmusik*) while my string quartet waited to board a New Jersey Transit train at New York City's Penn Station. Of course, our tuxedos and the flash-mob nature of our performance didn't hurt.

---

9. Weingarten, Gene. "Pearls Before Breakfast: Can one of the nation's great musicians cut through the fog of a D.C. rush hour? Let's find out." *Washington Post.* April 8, 2007.

I admired the artist's superlative performance, but he appeared to misunderstand some of the basic tenets of successful street performance. Instead of choosing a performance space where people necessarily need to stand and wait for a few minutes, the artist chose a transitional arcade. He positioned himself as far as possible from his passerby audience. People really had to go out of their way to listen or to donate.

While the artist is known to be quite mobile in performance, he stood rigidly still and barely moved, as if to avoid attention. In the same vein, he evaded his audience by hiding his face with a lowered baseball cap. He made no eye contact with his public. Most troublingly, the artist never appeared to acknowledge his benefactors or tell them, "Thank you!"

I consulted an expert, cellist Sean Grissom, who for decades has made the majority of his living busking in subways, parks, and public spaces. Sean plays everything from Bach and classical standards to pop, Cajun fiddling, rock, punk, and television show themes.

Sean deemed the *Washington Post's* busking escapade "a flawed experiment." In addition to the above points, Sean observed that unlike New York City, Boston, or New Orleans, Washington D.C. does not have structured public transit or street performance programs in place. Consequently, there is no culture or conditioning for passersby to donate. If a busking culture is not already in place, you have the added challenge of creating one.

In terms of what to do, Sean points out there are no one-size-fits-all rules. Any location does have potential as a successful spot. That said, where there is more traffic, your odds of attracting a crowd and getting donations improve. However, if you are in an area with extreme traffic flow, you may experience disappointing returns, if the crowd's momentum continually propels everyone forward.

According to Sean, you ideally should position yourself in areas where you are visible, accessible, but also safe, well illuminated, with your instruments and equipment "out of the line of fire." Many musicians prefer to have their backs to a wall or a post, to minimize blind spots, increase safety, and sometimes to get an acoustic boost. Your challenge is to create your performance space, as well as to be flexible enough to adjust or change locations if things don't seem to be working. One spot may work for one musician but not another.

Over time, Sean found that light amplification, his own high-quality backing tracks, and using a Boss Loop Station all contributed to better earnings. Any repertoire is fair game, as long as you play it well. Sometimes, a current chart-topper, a popular movie or television theme, or a song that captures the *Zeitgeist* may better catch people's attention. However, don't be afraid to focus on what you do best and enjoy the most.

Your own preferred repertoire may suggest a particular location. If you perform specific world music genres, consider playing in or near restaurants that serve that particular culture's cuisine.

Many savvy musicians who busk near arts centers play tunes from the shows, operas, and concerts that are being performed that night. Friends of mine who have "raked it in" playing purely instrumental classical music or jazz recommend busking in shopping or tourist areas. In these locations, people are unhurried, looking for entertainment, and most importantly, looking to spend money and time.

Logistics

While it's possible, simply, to hit the streets and give busking a shot, be aware that many towns may require street performers to have a permit. It's better to obtain one than to take your chances. Nobody wants to perform with anxiety over getting shut down or fined. Find out what's possible in your area, and take it from there. You may find that your local chamber of commerce, business improvement district, or arts council actually supports live performance. Busking is better if you do it with the support of your community.

CONSIDER THIS: BUSKING TIPS

Veteran New York City subway musician Sean Grissom raises some critical points for you to consider when you busk: "Commuters are going from Point A to Point B, and are NOT expecting, wanting, or needing your performance. How do you connect with them? How do you compete with their electronic media and other distractions of life? Busking is the opposite of a conventional stage performance where the audience wants to attend and participate in a performance. You somehow have to capture the attention of a non-captive audience. You have less than ninety seconds to grab their attention.

It is imperative for you to CONNECT with the people! You are there to provide a musical respite—for a very brief moment—from the stress of their everyday lives. Song selection, eye contact, stage presence, engagement (whether visual or verbal)—these are your tools.

As you perform, try out strategies. Some will work, some will not. What is empowering, though, is that you get immediate feedback, and you can adapt on the spot.

Hopefully, you will be rewarded with an 'addition' to your hat. Believe me, everything has made its way into my hat over the years, from Yankees tickets, to a used 'roach,' to a bag containing a bottle of Scotch and organic squash, to an extensive coin collection from all over the world. AND. . . I say 'THANK YOU!' to everyone who contributes."

CHAPTER 9

Audience Engagement and Cultural Ambassadorship

Music is powerful stuff. What else is central to birthdays, weddings, funerals, holidays, political events, rites of passage, ceremonies, and celebrations? What else can represent our highest achievements, proclaim our most profound beliefs, move us to tears, as well as inspire us to clap our hands and dance?

Music forms a central part of culture and identity, both globally and locally. Music's centrality to human civilization establishes it as a universal force that uniquely affirms our humanity and dignity. Is it any wonder that most significant social movements have included music and musicians who rallied around a cause?

As a musician, you have a role as a conveyor, preserver, and ambassador of culture. You help people to define and understand their own identities and experiences, as well as to consider those of others. You have a unique ability to get others to listen deeply, emotionally, and empathetically. Sharing music opens the door to sharing life.

"Sharing music opens the door to sharing life."

When we come to understand each other's music, we begin to understand each other's lives, communities, cultures, and perspectives. In one sense, any performance is an act of ambassadorship because you are presenting and sharing culture. In some situations, your listeners will already share your culture, so their identity and appreciation of it will be reaffirmed and reinforced. Other times, you will be in the role of helping others to understand a culture that is foreign or new to them.

FIG. 9.1. Evan Christopher of Eli Yamin Jazz Quartet Plays an Outreach Concert Outside Guatemala City on State Department Tour, 2015. Photo courtesy of Eli Yamin.

For eleven years, I gave educational concerts at one of the largest elementary schools in North America: PS 19 in Queens, NY. During that time, this highly international school served students representing forty-seven distinct nationalities and twenty-seven different native tongues.

Year after year, I marveled at how diverse the students were, yet how unified they were in expressing their love and appreciation for all of us performers and our music. We couldn't help but love and appreciate them, too. I wondered what I would learn if each of them spent an hour with us sharing their family's music. I pondered how a single piece of music can serve as a catalyst and means for genuine cultural dialogue.

As I began to participate and perform in international conferences and cultural exchange programs, I began to see firsthand the degree to which music can open minds, and in many cases, effect change.

Some years ago, I attended *The Concert for Pakistan*, a powerful concert at the United Nations' General Assembly Hall. Salman Ahmad, author of *Rock & Roll Jihad: A Muslim Rock Star's Revolution* (Free Press, 2014), had organized the event. Salman is also the lead guitarist and songwriter of Junoon, Pakistan's biggest rock band.

The concert served as a benefit for the UN High Commission for Refugees and to raise support for the three million Pakistani refugees who had been displaced by the Taliban and the war in Afghanistan. Salman used the evening as a platform for his message to unite people, fight bigotry and tyranny, promote peace, and help others.

He gathered many guest artists and speakers for the event, including Sting, Gwen Stefani, Melissa Etheridge, Deepak Chopra, and various political officials. During his performance, Salman shared contemporary cell phone videos, photographs, and personal narratives to underscore his urgent pleas for empathy, understanding, and aid. Advocating peaceful coexistence, he made a point to include Jewish and Christian musicians in his band that night.

Did the concert bring peace to the Middle East? Perhaps not, but everyone present received inspiration, an education, and a challenge to get involved and make the world a better place. Significantly, the event raised over a million dollars to aid Pakistan's internally displaced persons and rebuild girls' schools that the Taliban had destroyed.

When we consider the vastness of the world's problems, our humanitarian efforts as musicians can sometimes feel like a drop of water in the ocean. However, just as the oceans need every drop, humanity needs every note of every song. When you consciously engage your audiences and communicate your distinctive message, your impact exponentially increases. Never underestimate your power as an ambassador of culture and a purveyor of truth.

Application

What are some causes you feel passionate about? What are some charities that you support? Too often as performers, we focus solely on concerts that pay our bills and promote our own careers. Consider staging a benefit concert where you will donate all the proceeds to people or organizations that need it.

You will discover how quickly patrons, sponsors, collaborators, and volunteers will rally to your cause. Granted, organizing and publicizing any concert is no small task, and benefit concerts sometimes take extra effort because typically more people are involved and more is at stake. At the same time, the meaning, rewards, and personal benefits are often considerably greater than for-profit concerts.

Benefit concerts are always a great way to build community, make like-minded connections, reaffirm the purpose of your own art, and contribute to a greater cause.

OVERCOMING LANGUAGE BARRIERS

When you venture into international or cross-cultural performance, you will want to adapt your approach to accommodate your audiences' native or predominant tongue(s). Regardless of how you approach each situation, I strongly recommend that you speak at least a few words in your audiences' native language. At the minimum, learn how to say phrases like "Good evening!" and "Thank you!" You will be amazed at how strong of an impact just a few words in your audience's native language can make. You are acknowledging and affirming them. You are making efforts to communicate, and that encourages their efforts to listen.

At the most extreme end of the spectrum, you may choose to perform or present your entire concert in a language that you do not speak. If you have a host or actor to help narrate the concert, they can effectively deliver the majority of the verbal content.

Pianist and teaching-artist Jihea Hong-Park and I once designed an interactive duo concert for a New York Philharmonic *Learning Overtures* residency in Korea.

After we designed and scripted the entire concert in English, Jihea (fully bilingual) translated the script into Korean. While she assumed the leading role, she gave me quite a few strategic lines and interjections throughout. She made an audio recording of my lines, which I assiduously practiced. To be safe, we developed a few gestural cues so that I would not be entirely reliant on taking verbal cues in an unfamiliar language. It worked.

If you do have a basic understanding of another language's grammar and vocabulary, you will have a much easier time. Percussionist Justin Hines and I once performed as the featured guests in a monolingual concert scripted by student producers from Japan's Niigata University.

Among other things, we acted out an entire scene Kabuki-style. Because we both had informally studied Japanese for a few years, we understood every word of our scene, and were able to memorize and perform it almost as easily as if the script were in English. Investing time in learning another language is well worth your effort.

Performing a concert in a single tongue definitely makes for the most direct, efficient presentation. More commonly, though, you will find yourself in situations where bilingual presentation is preferred.

Working with an interpreter can take some getting used to. Be aware that effective translations in some languages may require more time and more words than you think. When I first gave concerts and lectures with live interpretation in Japan, I was warned that translations might take three times longer than my original statements. Though I had reduced my words and I had an efficient interpreter, I still occasionally spoke more than I should have.

Unless your audience truly understands your primary language, keep your sentences to an absolute minimum. You will be more effective if you speak shorter statements that are immediately translated than if you speak full paragraphs requiring lengthy translations.

Some artists performing in bilingual cultures manage to perform bilingual concerts without using an interpreter. They script their performances with primary speakers for each language. By embedding internal translation and context clues into their dialogue, the audience learns what each character is saying from the reactions of the character who speaks their native tongue.

If you are performing in a venue like Ottawa's National Arts Centre in Canada (a bilingual nation), the audience will receive program notes in both official languages. Larger venues generally have full-time translators to help with this, but consider contracting a translator for venues that do not. If you are seriously seeking to engage a bilingual culture, develop publicity materials in both languages.

BEING A MUSICAL AMBASSADOR

Eli Yamin

For five years, Eli Yamin, managing and artistic director of Jazz Power Initiative, served as Training Specialist for U.S. Department of State's The Rhythm Road: American Music Abroad. At the time, The Rhythm Road was hosted by Jazz at Lincoln Center, where Eli works as director of the Middle School Jazz Academy.

In addition to leading several tours with his jazz and blues bands, Eli worked with colleagues to design and deliver training sessions for fifty bands embarking on tours sponsored by the USDOS. Here's what Eli emphasizes when he prepares musicians for working globally as a musical ambassador.

Eli: Learn all you can about a culture where you are touring. This includes their language, music, literature, holidays, and major historical events, such as conflicts with other countries. It is very powerful when you acknowledge that you know some of this. Quote a favorite local poet. Reference an important landmark, or mention a good meal you were served. You can connect with a culture *through* its unique culture.

As you prepare your presentation, identify three strengths or distinctions from your band's repertoire, members, and style strengths.

For instance:

1. We play American roots music and feature the banjo.
2. Our band features men and women, each from different regions of our nation.
3. Some of us grew up with this music in our homes; others of us came to it later because we dug it.

Keep in mind these critical principles of audience engagement:

1. Show, don't tell.
2. If you do tell, tell a story.
3. Do interactive activities such as call-and-response singing, rhythmic clapping, and stomping.

Consider how your band's strengths align with the things you've learned about the culture you're visiting. Concerts provide great opportunities for making these connections overt. My band's blues shows often unfolded as an emotional narrative sprinkled with points of commonality between American traditions and those of our host countries.

Of course, sometimes, a simple universal human connection can be effective, for example: "We do this song for my Aunt Doris because her cooking is so good!" or "Duke Ellington wrote this song for his mother, so we'd like to dedicate this to all the mothers here!"

Remember to communicate emotionally. Your passion and commitment can cut through language barriers and cultural differences more than you can imagine.

Chelsey Green

Chelsey Green, leader of the contemporary jazz band Chelsey Green and the Green Project, has toured extensively through the U.S. Department of State's American Music Abroad program. Here are some of her words of practical wisdom as you prepare to be a musical ambassador.

Chelsey: Wherever you go, people will be excited to meet you and to hear your music. Be aware that audiences may have some preconceptions about how to interpret your genre.

In my own case, I had the unique opportunity to share contemporary, funk-inspired jazz with audiences and press representatives who considered jazz only to be "straight-ahead" (i.e., bebop and swing). Have an open ear to your listeners' perspectives, but know how to communicate your own interpretations as well. Commonalities help to bridge gaps.

Collaborate with local artists. One of the most rewarding parts of the international touring experience, musical collaborations can provide unique insight into your interpretation and stylistic approach.

Be ready to adapt quickly. The Green Project has a full rhythm section and uses amplification. Arriving at a venue with no equipment—or worse, no electricity—is the epitome of a "make-it-work" moment. The show must go on. When you find yourself in a similar position, quickly reconsider how to convey your musical message despite any limitations or obstacles.

Be aware of what's changing on the political landscape as you prepare your tour and as you are touring. A two-hour road trip may turn into a four-hour trip because you have to bypass protests in a particular area. (This actually happened to my group.) If you know what's going on, you can better adapt your musical presentation and effectively represent yourself in your interviews and media interactions.

As a cultural ambassador, you'll be doing a lot of traveling. A whole lot. Planes, vans, trains, buses, walking, and more. You'll be moving around different countries quite a bit, and you won't always have assistance with your bags and equipment. Pack light, but pack what you need.

Know the weather. Not only is this important for packing the right clothing and staying healthy, but it's also important for your instruments' care and well-being. You and your instrument need to last the entirety of the tour. Consider whether you need to bring humidifiers, dehumidifiers, or industrial-strength protection from rain or cold.

Take vitamins and rest. Rest days are built into your touring schedule for a reason. Rest on rest days. You'll need it. And don't put ice in your drink. Just, don't.

Definitely go sightseeing! Take advantage of the non-musical moments, too. It's such a beautiful opportunity to learn about and see a country through the eyes of a local. Don't get so caught up in the hustle and bustle that you forget to take time to appreciate the blessings. Be present in the moment and soak it in.

FIG. 9.2. Chelsey Green and the Green Project Working as Musical Ambassadors in Haiti. Photo Credit: Kevin Powe, Jr.

CHAPTER 10

Straightforward Answers to Common Questions

When I give interactive concert workshops and performances, most musicians express an appreciation for the ideas and strategies shared in this book. However, the thought of taking the information and applying it themselves often raises questions and concerns. Because you probably are wondering some of the same things, let's address the most common concerns.

If you've never done an interactive presentation before, how do you get started?

If you are excited about the possibilities and confident in your presentational abilities, go ahead and plan a wholeheartedly interactive event. If you feel a little cautious or unsure about interacting, start gradually.

If possible, perform with musicians who are successful with this approach. Let them take the lead, but ask to have an active role during the performance. If you are working on your own, try saying a few sentences before each piece. When that feels comfortable, include one to two simple audience-participation activities. As time goes on, you will become bolder and more comfortable.

How do you get good at this? I know some people who are naturals, but not everybody's good at this....

Interactive performance is a discipline and an art in its own right. As with musical performance, the skills and techniques must be learned, developed, and practiced. The more you practice, the better you become and the easier it gets.

> *"Interactive performance is a discipline and an art in its own right."*

You can also improve by studying other engaging performers. When I first began having residencies as a teaching artist, I relied heavily on the examples of experienced colleagues. I read their lesson plans, I adapted their best activities for my workshops, I asked them questions whenever I ran into problems. In short, I modeled my work after the best practices I knew.

When I was hired to stand in front of a full orchestra and lead an interactive concert, I viewed as many educational concerts as I possibly could. I watched videos of Leonard Bernstein's *Young People's Concerts*, Wynton Marsalis's *Marsalis on Music*, and other music education programs.

I attended events in public schools; I went to children's concerts by various organizations. I took notes on what worked and what bombed. I tried to ascertain why. I interviewed people who attended the events and studied their reactions. Whenever possible, I spoke to the producers of the event to find out their intentions and their assessment of the actual concert.

Learn from observing and analyzing best and worst practices. Granted, some people are more predisposed to this way of working than others. Fortunately, with a little effort, we all can improve our abilities, regardless of what our overall level is at the moment.

Application

One of the safest ways to interact is to take a successful activity, which you have observed, and lead it yourself. Go back to chapter 4 or read the transcripts in part IV (and online) to find ideas that you would feel comfortable trying. Try them out in a safe environment where failure isn't critical. Ask your family to be a "guinea pig" audience. Volunteer to perform at a senior center or your former elementary school. Practice.

A primary key to improvement is maintaining a commitment to lifelong learning. We must choose to keep getting better at engaging audiences throughout our careers, never settling for the ways we currently do things, and never assuming that what we do now is good enough. The field requires that we keep pressing forward so that we can share our art most effectively. We should model a life of ongoing inquiry and musical curiosity for our fellow musicians so that they, too, can improve.

If your concerns are mostly about speaking in front of a group, try taking a public speaking course or an acting course at your local community college. You can also join Toastmasters or other organizations devoted to honing speaking skills. Explore ways to interact with as few words as possible; many activities can be done without any words at all.

I believe in the interactive approach, but my group doesn't get it. They're impossible. How do I deal with them?

If I had a nickel for every time someone raised this issue…

There is no single solution to this problem; your plan of action must be tailored to the personalities and problems of your individual group. I will share a few success stories from colleagues in the field. (To protect the anonymity of the individuals, ensembles, and organizations, all the names have been changed.) Perhaps the solutions for their situations will apply to yours.

Rebecca was a member of a fairly large band that gave frequent performances in public schools, particularly middle schools. The senior members of the group favored a traditional lecture approach, which never seemed to connect with the students. On the way home, the ensemble would complain about how rotten today's youth are.

When Rebecca couldn't stand this pattern any longer, she told the group, "Look, let me lead the next concert, and let me do it my way. If it's a disaster, I'll take full responsibility, but give me the chance to experiment because the way we're doing things right now isn't working."

Rebecca was given carte blanche to design and host the next event. Because her approach proved a vast improvement over the status quo, the group gladly delegated responsibility for planning and scripting all audience engagement to her.

Rebecca felt she needed to use this confrontational approach because previously, she was not in a position of control or influence. If you find that you have no bearing on your group's concerts, you may need to assert yourself and offer to lead for a change.

Allison, a string quartet violist, had quite a different problem. She was the driving creative force behind her ensemble's interactive concert, and her first violinist was enthusiastic and supportive of everything she wanted to do. However, the second violinist and the cellist were, in her words, "Dead. They just sit there and act like they don't care about anything. I want to strangle them!"

The musicians in question were incredible players, but they had rarely given any performances outside of traditional recitals and concerts. Allison was taking them into totally unfamiliar territory, and they were understandably uncomfortable and reluctant to participate.

Allison solved her problems by enlisting help from outside of the group. She asked two qualified musician coaches to attend the dress rehearsal and provide feedback. The observers offered praise and constructive suggestions to all of the musicians. Non-threatening participatory roles were created for the reluctant partners. After the concert, the previously unforthcoming musicians came to appreciate Allison's approach, and they seemed open to trying similar events in the future.

If you struggle with disengagement within your group, sometimes an outside voice will prove effective in motivating unresponsive members.

Manny was frustrated by a group member who participated in counterproductive ways. "Every time we play a community concert, Edgar goes off on these long, boring biographies about the composer, or he gives these non sequitur monologues on stuff like 'why jazz is important.' It's so embarrassing, it makes the rest of us cringe!"

Manny's case is particularly complicated because his ensemble has a resident boor. Boors seldom realize that they are being boorish. There is no tactful way to alert them, nor is there any guarantee that they will believe you or behave any differently if you do.

One of the best ways to reign in boors and other verbal transgressors is to formally script your event, and hold all members to the script. If anyone balks, explain to him that your presentation has extremely limited time, and you want to make sure everything gets covered.

If your "Edgar" needs to have input into the script in order to feel personally validated, so be it. If his proposed text strays from your theme into less relevant areas, simply say something like, "That's great, Edgar, but we're getting away from the music here. I want to be sure that everything we do helps our audience to hear what comes next." If he digresses during the concert, try tactfully interrupting him with an interjection that keeps the group on course.

Film your concert. Watch and discuss it as a group. When people watch themselves, they often can see their own shortcomings more clearly than they can on stage. If possible, watch the video with someone outside of the group who hasn't seen the program before. Again, outsiders can provide input in ways that group members can't without jeopardizing group chemistry or relationships.

Stacy, an education director of a "big five" orchestra, found himself in a position where some members of his orchestra were philosophically opposed to any kind of interaction. As they saw it, audience-centered approaches turned the focus away from the orchestra and departed too much from the regular concertgoing experience.

Stacy listened to their concerns and undertook several initiatives to address them. To acknowledge the dissenting musicians' preference for more traditional ways of connecting with the public, he provided opportunities for them to give master classes, preconcert lectures, and post-concert talks. By doing so, he helped them to participate in outreach efforts that corresponded with their own views. Rather than ignore noncompliant individuals, Stacy made sure that every musician had a way to contribute successfully to the orchestra's education mission.

To test the validity of his interactive approaches, as well as the musicians' concerns, he hired an independent firm to formally poll audience members who had attended the interactive events. Over 75 percent of the audience members polled were enthusiastic about the new, interactive approach. Of the remaining 25 percent, roughly 3 percent responded negatively. Stacy presented the report to the orchestra committee, who consented that the new approach must be working.

I should mention that from the beginning, Stacy enlisted like-minded orchestra members to participate in his events and bolster support for his efforts. To effect philosophical change within an organization, you must have advocates and allies, as well as an ongoing, intra-ensemble communication plan for sharing the experiments and their impact. Little by little, institutional change can occur.

Jessica encountered Stacy's problem, but within a woodwind quintet. Two members violently opposed any audience participation; they preferred a presentational information-based approach, which Jessica often found condescending in tone. (For various reasons, she did not feel that she had the liberty to use the bold, take-control approach I previously described Rebecca using with her band.)

Jessica ultimately used a gradual, oblique strategy for steering her ensemble to a more audience-centered approach. She decided to perform a series of interactive recitals with her oboe and piano duo. She invited her quintet to attend, and little by little, they came to understand her ideas and perspective.

Currently, the quintet still gives fairly conventional community performances, but for each one, the quintet allows Jessica to lead one or two participatory activities. Although the performances are still not as interactive as Jessica would like, they are more so than they were two years prior.

What do you do if you find yourself in a really tough situation, like a school where the kids misbehave?

Sometimes, it's fun to sit around with musicians sharing our "nightmares from the field" in a game of "Can You Top This?" Every challenging situation demands a unique response, but usually there is a way to overcome (or at the minimum, survive) even the most challenging situations.

The first thing any group or organization should do is to take proactive measures to prevent a potentially bad situation. Put a reasonable cap on audience size. For children's concerts, require an appropriate number of adult chaperones. Have a nursery or a "cry room" for infants. Send participating organizations preparatory materials that include friendly information about the concert etiquette you expect. During the concert, abide by subtle control measures like saying, "I'm only going to pick volunteers who are sitting still and not calling out! . . . Oh, I love the way you're sitting quietly. You'll be our first volunteer!"

Also, check the attitudes of your colleagues, your ushers, and security guards. Do your voices and body language project warmth and enthusiasm, or do they exude fear, discomfort, disdain, or a wish that you were elsewhere? If anyone projects the latter attitudes, don't expect your audience to enjoy being with you.

> **CONSIDER THIS: RESPECT**
>
> Do your words treat the audience with respect, or are you unconsciously condescending or perpetuating unhealthy preconceptions and stereotypes? I once saw a performer tell an inner-city eighth-grade audience, "The bell's going to ring during this last number, but we'll keep playing. If you go out softly, you'll hear the end of it. Sneak out like you've just robbed a house!"
>
> A few students gasped incredulously, and others snickered and murmured. While the performer was probably trying to be "cool" or funny, his unfortunate remark insulted his audience by reinforcing implicit socioeconomic and racial prejudices.

Within your concert interactions, include control measures. Teach a quiet signal or use a conductor's cutoff signal. Be sure that the audience has settled down before you perform anything.

Even if your ensemble has an ideal attitude and preventative measures have been taken, behavior problems can still surface. Sometimes, the best response is to ignore the situation and let the appropriate authorities reprimand the offenders.

If no authority is present or competent, however, you may have to solve the problem yourself. During one performance, I encountered a fourth-grader on the front row who scowled, grimaced, and sat with his hands over his ears for the duration of the first piece. It became clear that this boy was determined to give a defiant performance of his own.

My next piece required a volunteer to play the drums. Instinctively, I selected the scowler when he volunteered. Instead of clowning, he took his role seriously, returned to his seat, and behaved for the rest of the concert. His misbehavior had apparently stemmed from an unspoken need for attention, and once I addressed it, he could function properly.

On occasion, an entire audience can get out of hand. Although I like to get audiences excited about music, I must be careful not to overexcite them. After one particularly fun activity with my band, the Doc Wallace Trio, a third-grade audience became a little too talkative and rowdy. Daniel Levy, the acoustic guitarist in my group, restored order by raising his hand and firmly saying, "We can't go on until everyone calms down." We waited patiently until the students regained their composure, then proceeded without problem.

How do you do interactive concerts for adults?

All of the strategies and ideas presented in this book can prove effective with virtually any audience. However, the way you present the material may need to be adjusted according to the age and the venue. Naturally, adults should be treated as adults. You should also assume that while some of them may have no formal musical knowledge, others may have extensive musical backgrounds.

In some venues, such as comedy clubs, the environment is so open and participatory that it would almost be strange or rude not to interact or experiment. Comedy showcases are particularly good places to try out five- to ten-minute self-contained performances in between acts. The instant feedback is incredible.

In a more staid environment (e.g., a recital hall) or a more social environment (e.g., a noisy club), you may need to adjust your approach. Unless adults bring children, they initially may be less prone to indulge in creative participatory activities, but if you establish your "out-of-the-ordinary" expectations from the beginning and win the audience over with a "low-threat" activity that has a significant payoff, you'll discover how readily people will adapt to your approach. Some types of activities will be more comfortable and conducive to particular venues than others.

The New World Symphony runs a series, *Inside the Music*, targeting young adult audiences. Concerts start early in the evening, last roughly an hour, and provide a "behind-the-scenes," in-depth exploration of a specific work, genre, or composer.

Successful themes have included:

- pairing their repertoire with food and drink
- teaching the audience to dance as an entry point to Latin music
- in-depth analytical approaches that served to unlock contemporary music
- using a performer's life, experiences, and personal photographs to highlight her direct connection to a genre that has particular meaning for her

When in doubt, ask yourself, "As a grownup, would I enjoy this event? Would I be excited to attend when I read the description?"

CONSIDER THIS: ENGAGING SHY ADULTS

Often adults prove shyer than children when it comes to answering or asking questions in front of others. Following a dress-rehearsal of an interactive performance designed for adults, a colleague commented on a particular phenomenon he has noticed: when we lead workshops and interactive performances for adults, our initial question is usually met by an awkward silence. Once that first question is answered, people participate more willingly.

As several of us confirmed that we shared the same experience, we wondered why this hesitation happens and what we could do about it. We concluded that this phenomenon stems from a couple of fairly obvious factors:

1. Nobody wants to appear foolish by giving a wrong or weird answer in front of a group of peers.
2. Having an expert ask for input from his audience is quite a departure from the traditional arts appreciation/lecture model. Consequently, it takes people a moment to adjust their expectations.

Out of our discussion some useful strategies for shortening the silence and increasing comfort with interaction emerged:

- Make your first question a "softball" (an easy question—probably one without wrong answers or one that requires no extensive expertise).
- Ask the first question in a way that it can be answered communally (e.g., by a show of hands or a unison verbal response).
- Poll the audience on their familiarity with the subject and set up a context for sharing. ("Raise your hands if this is your first encounter with the music of Thelonious Monk. . . . Okay, now raise your hands if you've heard a song or two of his or know a bit about him. . . . Now, raise your hands if you're a longtime Thelonious Monk fan. Good. Over the next half hour, we'll be drawing on each others' perceptions and expertise so that we all can hear what's great about this composer.")
- Frame the event differently to set up your expectations. To switch from a standard preconcert lecture to something more interactive, the Los Angeles Philharmonic set up microphones in the audience to suggest more of a talk-show environment. To take some of the formality and pressure off of the host as well as the audience, the event was titled a "Casual Talk," and the location was an open space where people could feel free to join the activities late.
- If adults are hesitating when you ask for something active like conducting, humming, or clapping, assure them that actively participating will make a big difference in their ability to hear and feel the music.
- Model the participation in a way that encourages people to join in.

In general, adults have a deeper hunger for information—particularly information on how the music works—and they expect interaction to be focused in a specific direction. Composer, pianist, and commentator Robert Kapilow has built quite a following with a lecture series called *What Makes It Great?* in which he and his performers thoroughly investigate a musical masterwork the day before a concert. Kapilow's audience is almost entirely adult, yet anyone attending can count on singing, taking part in musical experiments, or concentrating their utmost to meet the listening challenges that Kapilow gives. People keep returning and subscribing because Kapilow's participatory approach always helps listeners to discover details they would otherwise miss.

Application

Take an activity from a concert you have done for children, or choose an activity from a children's concert (see the transcriptions in part IV and online). How would you need to adjust the dialogue and the participation for an adult audience? For high school or middle school students?

I'd like to do this, but I'm overworked and can't find the time that it would take to revamp the programs I've been doing.

All of us are overworked, and none of us can find enough planning or practice time. Nevertheless, if we believe in the importance and relevance of audience interaction, we can make the time. If changing your approach is important to you, schedule time to work on it. Put pressure on yourself to follow through by booking and advertising an interactive performance. When a performance is pending, you can't avoid preparing.

To reiterate an earlier caution, when learning how to interact, don't undermine yourself and your self-confidence by under-preparing the interactive parts of your performance. Interactivity is challenging enough because it is unconventional; don't make it harder by winging it. Plan and rehearse. You will increase your success and confidence by starting simply, but with thorough preparation.

If your time constraints result from obligations to your employers, be honest with them. If they are asking you to do audience engagement, but not providing adequate time or compensation, make your needs known in a cooperative way that demonstrates your willingness and your commitment to outreach efforts. Stress how important it is to make the best impression on your audience. Some musicians have been granted brief sabbaticals for honing their presentational skills and designing concerts. Work with your employers to reach acceptable solutions.

How do you recommend bringing orchestral musicians on board when you're an education director or conductor who wants to involve them in interactive concerts?

Usually, every orchestra has a core group of musicians who are eager to participate in educational initiatives or who are enthusiastic about communicating musical ideas. Identify these musicians and bring them into your team. Some may prove to be excellent concert hosts, scriptwriters, or even concert producers.

Of course, this kind of involvement requires an extra measure of dedication, and it takes time to develop relationships with these musicians. Moreover, even the most enthusiastic musicians may need training or direction when starting out.

If the musicians are not primarily responsible for scripting and hosting the concert, but they have active roles to play, it is best to prepare a one-page outline that lets them know exactly what role to play at what time. The outline should clarify exactly what their participatory role is and when it happens. Go over the sheet in rehearsal, answer any questions, and be sure that each stand has a cue sheet for the concert. Outside of the rehearsal or during a break, speak individually to any musicians with significant roles. Orchestral musicians greatly appreciate efficient preparation and clear expectations.

Do we have to do something interactive for every piece of music?

Sometimes, after seeing a demonstration of a fairly involved activity, a musician nervously asks, "That was really sophisticated. Do we have to do something like that before every piece?"

Let's get something straight: interaction is a choice, not a compulsion. As concert designer, you can decide how much or how little to interact. You interact not because you "should" or "must," but because effective interaction vitalizes the experience of the audience.

> **"Interaction is a choice, not a compulsion. You interact not because you 'should' or 'must,' but because effective interaction vitalizes the experience of the audience."**

Some pieces benefit from a fairly involved setup. Other works, particularly short selections, are best served by a quick and simple introduction. Remember that it is also possible to lead one powerful activity that focuses the listening for the next few selections, or even an entire concert.

At least once during a performance, I like to let the audience hear something without any preparatory activity at all. The key is to find a balance within your concert. Arrange your repertoire and interactions in such a way that the activity order is as pleasing as the musical order.

If you're a highly interactive musician or a band, how do you get presenters to understand?

On the whole, presenters—especially for smaller, independent, and more regional venues—love to book performers who know how to engage their audiences. Some presenters now require any artists to speak to audiences in addition to performing an evening of music.

Performers and ensembles who interact effectively bring an extra dimension to their performances. Use your skills as an asset. Mention them in your press kit and publicity materials. Make your manager or agent aware of what you can do.

Interaction is best understood through experience, not description. If you can give a short demonstration that includes a brief preparatory activity and a performance, presenters will know exactly what you are offering, and they will buy it. Put together a five- to ten-minute video compilation of your best audience interactions, and film a few complete interactive concerts for sharing.

When you choose to make presenters aware of your intentions may depend on the situation. Often, interaction is a selling point, but if you sense you are dealing with conventional or conservative bookers, you may initially choose to hint at what you do, and reveal the full concept gradually. Appealing to familiar artists who do similar work can help hesitant presenters to feel secure.

These techniques are great; can you tell me how to use them in other areas, like teaching private lessons or ensembles?

Most of the techniques presented in this book can be easily transferred to teaching situations, because so much of the approach originated in classrooms and schools. When we apply these strategies to instrumental teaching, we and our students can benefit from an enriched appreciation for the music we are studying.

I think one of the major reasons for student attrition in private lessons and school ensembles is that students grow bored with rehearsing the same music over and over. When the focus becomes so centered on perfect execution, it's easy to forget what's great about the music.

Try developing some creative teaching approaches by following the activity-design procedure that we discussed in chapter 3. Study the piece, find an entry point, and design activities appropriate for your learners.

When helping private students, look for ways to help them explore a concept or solve a musical problem in a creative way. Whenever possible, engage multiple intelligences and different learning styles.

> **CONSIDER THIS: ENGAGEMENT IN PRIVATE LESSONS**
>
> In private lessons, students sometimes benefit from an approach that departs from traditional pedagogy and addresses an intelligence other than musical intelligence. When I was in graduate school, I had the privilege of assisting Karen Tuttle with a very gifted studio of Juilliard violists. Grace, a master's student, approached me for help with Zoltán Kodály's transcription of J.S. Bach's *Chromatic Fantasy*—one of the most technically challenging pieces in the viola repertoire.
>
> Grace had mastered all of the technical challenges of the piece, but she felt her performance was not as musically interesting as she would like. Rather than go through the piece and dictate my own interpretation, I asked her to choose a section that she particularly wanted to improve.
>
> After she selected a passage of ascending and descending arpeggios, I handed her a blank sheet of paper and asked her to sketch the melodic contour with a magic marker. When her graphic notation was finished, I asked her to improvise music that followed the shape of the contours. The only rule I imposed was that she couldn't use any of Bach's notes.
>
> When she was comfortable interpreting the contours by improvising scales and arpeggios, I asked her to take the next step of writing various moods, dynamics, and emotions for each line. After improvising and experimenting with the various options, she returned to Bach's original and played her chosen passage with spirit and emotional flair. Our experiments away from the piece had sharpened her sense of the musical possibilities within Bach's sweeping arpeggios.

Students in orchestras, bands, and choirs enjoy using their instruments and voices in creative, exploratory ways. Some directors nurture students' musical interest by taking one or two Fridays a month to lead a workshop related to one of the pieces that's being performed. For examples of the kinds of workshops you could lead, see the New York Philharmonic's *Special Editions for Teachers*.[10]

---

10. See annotated bibliography for citations for *An American Celebration, Bernstein Live,* and *Pathways to the Orchestra.*

Does every performance have to be interactive?

As King Solomon said, "To everything, there is a season and a time for every purpose under heaven." In every situation, you will need to decide for yourself how much or how little to interact, as well as the best way to do so.

Every performance is a transaction between performers and listeners. Some concerts, like major debuts, have traditionally maintained a very formal delineation between the two. But let me make a case for breaking the "fourth wall."

When you interact with audiences, you influence your listeners' perceptions and concert experiences. This includes the opinions of critics, members of the press, and prospective managers or talent scouts who are in attendance.

International violin soloist Rachel Barton Pine firmly believes in and practices audience engagement techniques. For a major New York recital, she chose an ambitious and athletic program consisting of Niccolò Paganini's complete *24 Caprices for Solo Violin* with her own "Introduction, Theme, and Variations on *God Defend New Zealand*" as an encore.

Rachel carefully prepared and scripted her program by grouping the caprices in sets of two or three. Between each set, she shared contextual details or revealed insider secrets about each piece's challenges or musical underpinnings. Often, she treated the audience to a brief thematic, technical, or interpretive demonstration, sometimes sung. In addition to performing the caprices with consummate artistry, she impressively led her audience to perceive each one as a unique and fascinating gem.

When *The New York Times* published its thoroughly positive review, a majority of the details and content was quoted verbatim or paraphrased from Rachel's narration and audience interactions. By engaging her audience, Rachel also directly engaged the critic, who in turn penned a thoughtful, detailed, and warm review.

> **CONSIDER THIS: RACHEL BARTON PINE**
>
> Violin virtuoso Rachel Barton Pine has this to say about the positive effect of audience engagement on her Paganini complete caprices program:
>
> "When I first started performing Paganini's complete twenty-four caprices in a single evening's concert, I did it without any talking or interaction. Just getting through the notes was enough of a challenge."
>
> "Audience members were appreciative, but frequently commented that it was a long evening of a lot of works that all sounded kind of the same. After I finally started sharing what I feel makes each caprice different and special, the reactions became the exact opposite: people said that they were astonished by Paganini's incredible variety! Here's the amazing thing: I hadn't changed my interpretations at all!"
>
> As this story makes clear, audiences' perceptions can be greatly influenced by your choice to interact (or not). Rachel's love of Paganini's caprices and her skill in interpreting them remained constant. Once she adopted a more personal approach and gave her audiences entry points to the caprices, listeners could share the same love and exquisite appreciation for detail that Rachel enjoys as an artist.

Interaction increases your odds of connecting with your listeners. By breaking down the imaginary wall between you and your audience, listeners get to know and appreciate who you are as a human being. With few exceptions, people enjoy this relationship, and they are more likely to become loyal fans.

> *"Interaction increases your odds of connecting with your listeners."*

While the purposes of some performances suggest more interactivity than others, every performance should seek to engage the audience and heighten its musical perceptions. Interactive approaches simply give you more exciting options for accomplishing this objective.

Assess each situation individually. With experience, you'll know what's right.

CHAPTER 11

Engagement Is a Mindset

Occasionally, musicians wax nostalgic about a time when there were music teachers, instrumental programs, and performing ensembles in practically every school. Sometimes, the wistfulness gives way to resentment about the extra demands made on musicians as presenters and arts organizations seek to fill the educational voids. Some musicians maintain that if music education (or fundraising, marketing, and government support) was everything it should be, professional musicians could be relieved of the need to learn the art of audience engagement. This view raises an important question: If we had better, more universal music education in this country, would interactive performances still be necessary?

Absolutely. Even if effective music education programs are in place (may they ever be!), artists cannot afford to shirk their responsibility to reach out to audiences. Remember, during the golden age of music education in America, Leonard Bernstein still sensed a profound need to educate and cultivate audiences. Judging from the vivid reminiscences of those who grew up on Bernstein's concerts, his efforts were well spent.

Moreover, popular and contemporary music styles evolve quickly. This week's favorite artist may be passé in less than a year. Longevity depends on communicating with your fan base, building a following, and continually engaging new listeners.

Research from the Lila Wallace Foundation concludes that the future of the arts depends on changing our sense of what participation in the arts means.[11] The foundation recommends that artists:

1. deepen the experience of the existing arts-goers
2. broaden their contact with people who are like current arts-goers
3. diversify to include new kinds of people in their audiences

Interactive performance is one of the rare ideas that can accomplish all three objectives at the same occasion. Interaction can deepen the level of engagement of sophisticated audiences, broaden the appeal to make newcomers feel successful, and engage diverse audiences through the universal effectiveness of hands-on understanding.

> *"Interaction can deepen the level of engagement of sophisticated audiences, broaden the appeal to make newcomers feel successful, and engage diverse audiences through the universal effectiveness of hands-on understanding."*

Clearly, we cannot depend on others to build relationships between us and our audiences. To build these relationships, we must interact; we must engage.

Ideally, engagement is more than a performance strategy; it's an approach to life. The more adept we become at sharing our music with others, the more we will realize that we have daily opportunities to be advocates and ambassadors for our art. Some of the most inspired musicians I know seek to have musical conversations with total strangers. Others get out their instruments to demonstrate them for inquisitive children who are riding on the same train car. To these musicians, everybody is a potential listener, music-lover, subscriber, board member, private student, or colleague.

---

11. Walker, Chris and Stephanie Scott-Melnyk with Kay Sherwood. *Reggae to Rachmaninoff: How and Why People Participate in Arts and Culture*. Washington D.C.: The Urban Institute, 2002.

We are in the communication business. With our instruments and voices, we convey some of humankind's deepest passions and innermost thoughts. Unless we learn to present our music with the same artistry, integrity, and creativity with which we perform it, its substance may not be appreciated or understood by everyone in our audiences.

To fully communicate, we must engage our audiences in ways that heighten their perceptions and emotions. We must formulate long-term plans for cultivating musical understanding and for developing and maintaining relationships with the audiences in our communities. Nobody else is going to do it for us.

If we rise to the challenge creatively, however, our responsibility becomes a joy, not a burden. As we seek to convey the greatness of a musical work, we immerse ourselves in the work and rediscover its greatness for ourselves. How wonderful it is to return to pieces we have performed for years and formulate new insights or notice details we had previously overlooked. How incredible it is when we enable an audience to listen with the same sense of awe and discovery!

As we learn to interact in meaningful ways, our musical understanding grows with our audience's. We help our listeners to hear our insights. They help us to hear theirs. We revisit our repertoire with new perspectives and intriguing questions, and the cycle continues.

Our capacity to share music with our audiences is in direct proportion to our own musical curiosity and passion. If we cultivate these two faculties, we shall always have something to communicate, we shall always maintain our musical enthusiasm, and we shall always have a fervor for helping others to hear. Our audiences will truly listen, and we will never settle for anything less.

PART IV

Concert Transcriptions

No book on audience engagement would be complete without real-life transcripts of concerts that worked. Included are eight transcripts (one here in the book and seven more online), which illustrate the primary types of interactive concerts you are likely to design: concerts about composers, inquiry-driven concerts focused on developing listening skills and musical understanding, and thematic concerts with natural curricular ties to learning and literacy standards. Regardless of its overall theme, each concert seeks to illuminate specific repertoire through strategic activities.

These transcripts represent performances for a variety of audiences at considerably different venues. The activities and dialogue vary accordingly; hopefully, you will get a clear sense of what interaction looks like under different circumstances. The introduction to each concert explains its particular context.

To access seven additional transcripts, go to www.halleonard.com/mylibrary, and enter the code printed on the first page of this book.

Application

After you have read through the transcripts, reexamine them. What entry point is chosen for any given piece? What activity gave the audience an experience of it? What are some other possible entry points and activities? What interactive archetypes are used? Are there new strategies that weren't mentioned previously? The more you analyze the choices an interactive performer makes, the better you'll become at understanding and applying your own interactive skills.

NOTE: All of the scripts are protected by copyright law, but if you are interested in performing all or part of a particular concert, a license can be arranged.

CHAPTER 12

Improvisational Journey

Improvisational Journey is a solo concert I designed for myself and my own preferred repertoire. Although this concert began in elementary schools, I present it here as an example of an evening-length interactive concert suitable for a "grown-up" audience. Over dozens of performances, the concert has had several incarnations with varied formats, repertoire, and activities—most of which appear here. This transcript is drawn from multiple performances, but for convenience, it shall be presented as though it all happened at the place where my own interactive journey began: Saginaw, Michigan.

The concert was held at St. Stephen's Church, a Catholic church with modern architecture and reverberant but clear acoustics. Seating is on one level in a somewhat semicircular pattern, and sightlines are excellent throughout the sanctuary. The space accommodates approximately five hundred people. Multiple aisles give easy access to various parts of the sanctuary.

As you read, keep an eye out for various connections that were made to people in the community. Even if you are "just one musician," your residencies can involve far more people and organizations than you might first imagine.

IMPROVISATIONAL JOURNEY
Musicians:
David Wallace, viola, violin, and piano
Luis Millán, guitar
The Saginaw Bay Youth Orchestra Chamber Group

Improvisation with Audience
J.S. Bach: "Prelude in C Major"
David Wallace: *Black-Key Improvisation*
Heinrich Biber: *Passacaglia "The Guardian Angel"*
Georg Philipp Telemann: *Viola Concerto in G Major*

Intermission

Niccolò Paganini: "Caprice No. 24"
Two Rounds of Texas-Style Contest Fiddling
George Gershwin: "Summertime"
Leroy Jenkins: "Viola Rhapsody," "Big Wood," "Festival Finale"

Spoken introduction from Scott Seeburger of Dow Corning and the Saginaw Community Enrichment Commission:

> [Enter from the back of the hall, and without speaking, use body percussion to get the audience to perform layered rhythm patterns in the tempo of the Bach "Prelude in C Major." Pass out percussion instruments to volunteers who improvise rhythms over the layers. (Model it by jamming on each instrument while seeking a volunteer to take the instrument.) Add in melodic vocal patterns if desired, and begin melodic improvisation in C on viola. Build the piece to a satisfying climax and conclusion. Youth orchestra musicians collect the instruments during applause.]

DAVID: Good evening! Tonight we're going to take a journey into the world of musical improvisation. As we explore music spanning over three hundred years, we'll discover the different shapes improvisation can take. But first, I'm going to ask you, "What is improvisation?" How would you define it?

ADULT 1: It's when you make something up off the top of your head.

DAVID: So, it's an act of spontaneous creation.

ADULT 1: Yes.

DAVID: Who can add to that?

ADULT 2: It could be like in jazz when a musician does a solo on a 32-bar song.

DAVID: Tell me more about the solo part.

ADULT 2: Well, the rest of the band is playing the changes, but the person doing the solo is improvising on the chords or the melody.

DAVID: Ah, so there may be a background structure that underpins an improvisation. And one person may be featured while the others support him?

ADULT 2: Yes.

DAVID: And in the front row, what do you have to tell us?

CHILD 1: There can be variations or decorations like ornaments, and lots of times, the audience claps to show that something's good.

DAVID: Great! What's your name?

CHILD 1: Catherine.

DAVID: Catherine, where did you learn all that?

CHILD 1: You came to my school and told us.

DAVID: Thank you for paying such close attention! Would you like to help me host the rest of the concert?! [Laughter]

All that's been said is true. Improvisation is about creating in the moment, whether the improvisation is very free or highly structured. We began the evening by spontaneously creating a piece. Some of us were repeating very regular patterns, which we changed every now and then, and others were left to their own inspirations when they were given instruments. But in truth, we didn't know exactly what we would create. That's partly what makes improvisation exciting: not knowing exactly where the journey is going to take you.

In the Baroque period, which lasted roughly from 1600 until 1750, musicians understood how exciting it was to begin an event with an improvised piece of music. It was expected that musicians would begin a church service or a dance with an improvisation called a "prelude." In time, many musicians actually began to write their preludes down, so we have a good idea of what these improvisations sounded like. I'm going to use my viola to perform the prelude from the *Cello Suite No. 3 in C Major* by Johann Sebastian Bach. This is how our evening might have begun if it were 1720, and I was the improvising musician preparing us for an evening of dance.

[**Perform "Prelude in C" on Viola.**]

DAVID: Although there's always an element of freedom and fantasy in Baroque preludes, you can hear that there's also a sense of order and structure.

[**The following is punctuated with excerpts from the prelude.**]

In this prelude, Bach is mostly playing around with scales—specifically, scales in the key of C major . . . or when he's not playing scales, he's outlining harmonies. . . . Sometimes, he modulates to different keys—like he's taking us to a different setting or feeling . . . and sometimes, he's just letting me show off a cool bowing technique. . . .

So even within genres that suggest free improvisation, it's evident that musicians usually will focus on a handful of ideas and develop them one at a time within a given context. Now, I'm going to show you how *you* can do it.

How many of you have a piano or a keyboard instrument at home? I'll let you in on a secret that will enable you to improvise your own piano preludes. If you only play the black keys, you can never play a wrong note. Never! To prove that point, I'm even going to use my entire arm at some points to press about fifteen black keys at once. As long as you stay on the black keys, whatever you play will sound great. If you find a rhythm or a melody you like, do it again or change it a little until your fingers lead you to a new idea.

It can help if you have an idea about the larger structure, like knowing the feeling you want to express or thinking about what you want to do in terms of style or tempo. So, I want you to give me some parameters for my "Black Key Improvisation." Let's plan a scheme for the tempo. Contrast is always good, so I'd like to include sections of both fast and slow music. Who can suggest a plan for the tempos of the piece?

ADULT 3: Start slow, then gradually build it until it's as fast as possible.

DAVID: And how should it end?

ADULT 3: With one big crash.

DAVID: Okay. So here we go . . . slow-fast black-key improvisation culminating in one big crash!

[Perform "Black Key Improvisation" on piano.]

DAVID: So you can see that just with one or two little rules—like stay off the white keys, and gradually build the tempo—it's possible to improvise an interesting piece of music. The next time you find yourself at a piano, try this experiment. You'll be surprised what you discover.

Free spontaneous creation is one end of the improvisation spectrum, but more often than not, improvisation happens within a set structure. One of the oldest and most common ways to improvise is to make up melodies over a repeating bass line. You can hear this in jazz, blues, or in an old dance from the Spanish baroque called the "passacaglia." Could everyone say "passacaglia"?

ALL: Passacaglia!

DAVID: Good. In a *passacaglia*, there's a bass line that repeats over and over, and while that melody is repeating over and over, there's a lot of cool stuff that happens around that melody. But to really show you how a passacaglia works, we're going to create one together. Let's get a beat going!

[Begin snapping a steady beat, then begin singing C-B♭-A♭-G on the syllable "da," and indicate for the audience to join in. They continue singing while I improvise variations above them.]

DAVID: Great singing! Let's give our improvised passacaglia a title . . . who can suggest a name?

ADULT 4 (singing on the bass line): Down . . . the . . . moun- . . . tain!

DAVID: Nice. The "Down the Mountain" passacaglia by the Saginaw Community Singers and artist-in-residence. The passacaglia I'm about to perform for you has a title, too: "The Guardian Angel." What's a guardian angel?

ADULT 5: It's someone who protects you.

DAVID: Is that a full-time or a part-time job?

ADULT 5: Full-time, I hope!

DAVID: Full-time. In this passacaglia, that melody you all were singing, "da-da-da-da," represents the continuous ongoing presence of the guardian angel. It's always there. Sometimes, it may be hard to hear it because of all the variations that are happening around it, but it's always there. So, if that melody is the guardian angel, what do you think the other music might represent?

ADULT 6: Evil.

ADULT 7: The devil.

ADULT 8: Temptation or trials.

ADULT 9: Danger.

ADULT 10: The life of the person who's being protected.

DAVID: So, if you were a composer or improviser trying to represent the evil, danger, or temptations of a person going through life, what kinds of qualities would you want that music to have? What would it sound like?

[**Write the suggestions down on a chart.**]

ADULT 11: Dark, minor . . . dissonant chords.

DAVID: So, harmonies with a dark, unsettled, or clashing quality.

ADULT 12: I'd want plenty of contrasts.

DAVID: Like what kind of contrasts?

ADULT 12: Sometimes loud, sometimes soft. Sometimes fast, sometimes slow. Lots of surprises.

DAVID: What else?

ADULT 13: I'd have a lot of things going on at the same time to make it feel chaotic.

DAVID: Good. I'm going to perform "The Guardian Angel" passacaglia for you, and I'd like you to do two things. First, see if you can hear the guardian angel "da-da-da-da" melody. No matter how much is going on, it's *always* there, except for one place where it stops, and I improvise a short solo called a "cadenza." Second, notice all the different ways the music shows all the trials, dangers, and temptations of the person's journey. Here's "The Guardian Angel" passacaglia written in 1675 by the German violinist and composer Heinrich Biber.

[**Perform Biber's passacaglia.**]

DAVID: So, let's see a show of hands: how many of you heard the guardian angel melody most of the time except for during the cadenza? . . . and how many could hear it all the time? Great. And what were some of the ways Biber showed a person going through all of life's dangers, evils, and temptations?

ADULT 14: Some really fast notes!

DAVID: Absolutely [plays a measure of a fast variation and adds "fast notes" to the list]. What else?

ADULT 15: Sometimes, it was actually very soft and comforting.

DAVID: Yes, almost as though the person finds security in the presence of the angel. [Plays a softer variation and adds the new thought to the list.] Let's go through the rest of our predictions. Did we hear dark, minor, or dissonant chords? Contrasts in volume and tempo? Surprises? Many things going on to suggest chaos? Excellent. So you can see how much possibility there is for creating music above a repeating bass line, and that's why it's been a favorite technique of improvising musicians for centuries.

So, we began our concert by exploring essentially free improvisation, then we experienced improvisation over a bass line, and now, we'll move to one of the most structured forms of improvisation: ornamentation. As the name suggests, ornamentation is really about decorating pre-existing melodies by improvising embellishments. This was a widespread practice in Bach and Biber's day; it was rare for musicians to perform the music exactly as it was written.

[Members of the Saginaw Bay Youth Orchestra Chamber Group walk onstage.]

I'm going to play a few ornaments, and I'm going to ask you to draw a shape in the air that represents the sound of the ornament. Here's a popular ornament called a *trill* . . . I see some of you doing zigzag lines; some composers actually used that symbol to show a trill . . . Here's another one—a very quick, sharp kind of trill called a *mordent*. Let's see how you would draw that. Look around, and see what you see others doing. Here's another ornament called a *turn*. And sometimes, musicians would just decorate a melody with passing notes and scales.

Luis Millán and the Saginaw Bay Youth Orchestra Chamber Group are joining me now. We're going to perform the *Viola Concerto in G Major* by Georg Philipp Telemann. This was written in 1730, and to our knowledge, it's the world's first solo viola concerto. It was quite possibly the first instance of a violist getting to stand in front of an orchestra and improvise.

You probably noticed all these giant, decorated Telemann viola concerto scores we've posted on the walls of the church. As I toured the schools, during each concert, I would play an unornamented version of the first movement of this concerto while a few students decorated the score of it with artwork and the kinds of ornamentation symbols you were drawing in the air. Then I would repeat the movement again, using these decorations as a springboard for my improvised ornaments. [Pointing to a wildly decorated version.] This version was particularly challenging!

So, if I just take the first solo viola phrase and play it without any ornamentation, it sounds like this. [Play the opening line of the viola solo.] But when I read this decorated score and play it with these butterflies and curlicues, it sounds like . . . [play ornamented version].

Is there a student here who remembers what we talked about when we compared the ornamented version to the unornamented version?

CHILD 2: The first way was like a cake without frosting, and second way was like a cake with frosting.

DAVID: And which one did you like better?

CHILD 2: The second one!

DAVID: Me too. Tonight, I'll be taking the best ideas from the decorated scores that you see, and use them as a basis for my improvised ornaments as we perform Telemann's *Viola Concerto in G Major*. Keep your ears open for moments where the orchestra stops and I have to improvise a cadenza. Enjoy!

[**Perform Telemann** *Viola Concerto in G Major.*]

DAVID: We're going to take a ten-minute intermission, but don't go away because when you come back, we'll take improvisation out of the German baroque and into the realm of violin pyrotechnics, Texas-style fiddling, and jazz! Let's have one more round of applause for Luis Millán and the brilliant young musicians of the Saginaw Bay Youth Orchestra Chamber Group!

> [Intermission. As the lights dim, enter from the wings and perform Paganini's "Caprice 24" and travel through audience.]

DAVID: That was the 24th caprice of Italian violinist Niccolò Paganini, who was such an amazing violinist and improviser that he was rumored to have sold his soul to the Devil in exchange for his incredible talent. As he toured Europe, he often would include an improvised theme and variations as part of his concert or as an encore. He would take a popular melody—a *theme*—and then play several different versions of it. Mozart, Haydn, and Beethoven had done this before him, so it really wasn't a new concept, but what was new was some of the special effects he could make on his violin.

Let's break down what he did. Everybody here knows "Yankee Doodle," right? [Play "Yankee Doodle" melody.] I'm going to use that for my theme. Now, let's make up some variations based on some of the innovative effects you heard in the 24th caprice. What was something that you noticed me doing in the caprice?

ADULT 16: There was that plucking part.

DAVID: Yes, he did a pizzicato, or plucking variation. If we did something similar in "Yankee Doodle," it would sound like this [demonstrate]. What else did you hear?

ADULT 17: I heard an almost violent part where you were going like **(gestures)**.

DAVID: (Plays the beginning of the triple stop variation.) Like this?

ADULT 17: Yes.

DAVID: That would be chords. If we do that to "Yankee Doodle," you would get . . . **(play chordal variation on "Yankee Doodle")**. What else did you hear?

ADULT 18: There were some fast scales.

DAVID: Yes, almost like he had taken a lesson from Heinrich Biber's passacaglia. If we put some fast scales into a "Yankee Doodle" variation, you might have something like . . . [**improvise fast scalar variation**]. Let me show you one other technique where he lightly touches the string to make ultra-high-pitched sounds called *harmonics* [**demonstrate a phrase of the harmonics variation**]. If I do that to "Yankee Doodle," you'll hear something like . . . [**play harmonics variation**]. So, I'm going to make up a short Paganini-style theme and variations on "Yankee Doodle." First, I'll play the melody, then I'll play a pizzicato variation, a chords variation, a variation with fast scales, a harmonics variation, and maybe one or two more for good measure. Here we go. . . .

[**Perform a theme and variations on "Yankee Doodle."**]

DAVID: Now, let's hear Paganini's 24th caprice again, but this time, listen to it as a series of variations, each based around a particular technique.

[**Perform "Caprice 24."**]

DAVID: I'm going to invite guitarist Luis Millán back to the stage to join me for this next segment, and we're going to perform two rounds of Texas-style contest fiddling. I grew up in Texas where they have a very rich musical tradition that grew out of competitions where people would come from all over the nation to prove who was the best fiddler. Texas-style fiddling includes many of the improvisational techniques we've explored tonight, and it's a particularly interesting style because it is a melting pot of genres and improvisational techniques from around the world.

Most of the fast tunes are variations that happen over a repeated bass line. [**LUIS performs a 16-bar walking bass progression in A major with jazz harmonies.**] It's a little jazzier and more complex than Biber's "guardian angel" theme, but it serves the same function.

I'll be using quite a bit of ornamentation, only instead of being the kinds of ornaments you would find in the German baroque, I'll play [**punctuate with demonstrations of each**] trills . . . rolls . . . graces . . . and triplets derived from Irish and Scottish fiddling.

And while I'll be creating variations, instead of using Paganini's pyrotechnic techniques, I'll be using techniques that developed in American fiddling like fourth-finger drones . . . or creating variations in a higher position . . . or adding in some jazzy blue notes.

Now, so far, you've been a very polite audience, and have listened very well and attentively, but I'm going to ask you to behave like an audience at a Texas fiddle contest. At a fiddle contest, when a performer does something really interesting, the audience will spontaneously applaud or yell encouragement.

Let's practice. Let's say you were really impressed with a variation I just played, so you decide to applaud for about five seconds . . . ready? Go! Alright, now let's do that again, but yell, "Whoo!". . . .

Wonderful! Now let me just hear you say, "Hey-hey! Yeah!". . . Good! I think you're ready.

Make me work for your cheers, though. Don't respond unless you hear something really great, and only do it a couple of times per tune.

We'll play you two contest rounds. At a Texas-style fiddle contest, you're required to play three tunes per round: a *breakdown* (which is basically a very jazzy, improvisatory reel), a *waltz*, and a tune of choice *other* than a breakdown or waltz. The tune of choice may be a polka, a schottische, a hornpipe, a swing tune, a rag, or none of the above. So, here's a contest round. The breakdown will be "Tom & Jerry," the waltz is "Wednesday Night Waltz," and the tune of choice will be a quick, Mexican polka called "Jesse Polka."

[Perform contest round 1.]

DAVID: Thank you! We're going to play another round, since it sounds like we passed that one! The breakdown for the second round will be "Billy in the Lowground," which goes all the way back to seventeenth-century Scotland. There's a story—probably apocryphal—that there was a farmer named Billy who was farming the lowlands by the river, and he fell into a deep pit. For some reason—don't ask me why—he happened to have his fiddle with him. The variations represent his fiddling for help.

While you listen to this breakdown, I'd like you to notice another element of the Texas style. One thing that distinguishes it from bluegrass and other folk styles is that the improvisation is really driven by a 3+3+2 cross rhythm. Instead of going **ta**-*ka-ta-ka,* **ta**-*ka-ta-ka* like most fiddle music or classical music, it subdivides the beat with a jazzy rhythm: **ba**-*da-da,* **ba**-*da-da,* **dee**-*da!* **One**-two-three, **one**-two-three, **one**-two! Try that: **ba**-*da-da,* **ba**-*da-da,* **dee**-*da!*

[**Have the audience loop the cross-rhythm and then play a phrase or two over it.**]

That's the basic groove. You could hear when I added melody that I was often looping three-note patterns with you; that's what's called a *riff.* And in Texas, they love to riff on this breakdown. Here's "Billy in the Lowground."

[**Peform "Billy in the Lowground."**]

DAVID: Next, we'll play a Canadian waltz that is usually called—oddly enough—"Canadian Waltz." The original name was actually "Ookpik Waltz." *Ookpik* is an Inuktitut word for "snowy owl." The waltz itself is rather somber because it uses some blue notes and the kind of ornamentation that you might find in Scottish airs and ballads.

[**Perform "Canadian Waltz."**]

We'll finish the round with a ragtime tune that was originally a piano rag by Iowan composer George Botsford: the "Black and White Rag." You'll really hear the **ba**-*da-da,* **ba**-*da-da,* **dee**-*da!* cross-rhythms in this one. Every now and then, Luis is going to stop, and I'll play a short solo called a *break.* Breaks were common in early jazz and swing. They're similar to the baroque cadenzas you heard in the Biber and the Telemann, only this time, they're very rhythmic and happen in the span of four beats. In the school concerts, the kids got to improvise breaks in the moment, but tonight, I'll do the honors.

[**Perform "Black and White Rag."**]

DAVID: Thank you. We're going to continue in a jazzy vein with a standard that is a favorite of Texas fiddlers and jazz musicians alike: George Gershwin's "Summertime." As someone mentioned at the beginning of the concert, jazz musicians will often improvise a solo over the chord changes of a song. The solo may be based on the melody, or it may depart from it. In a band situation, everybody takes a solo, but first, the tune is presented by the singer or a melody instrument, and usually at the end the tune comes back as well.

Since I'm sure most of us know the song, let's sing the first verse together, then Luis will take a solo, I'll take a solo, then let's finish with the second verse. Luis?

[LUIS plays intro; perform "Summertime" as a sing-along.]

DAVID: I'm going to finish tonight's concert with a set of pieces by Leroy Jenkins, who was one of the pioneers of avant-garde jazz violin. I moved to Brooklyn about a year ago, and by a miraculous coincidence, my new home was only a few doors down from Leroy's. He stopped me on the street one day and said, "Hey, are you that violinist who lives on Prospect Place? . . . Come on over sometime, and I'll show you some tunes!"

The first piece I'm going to perform is called "Viola Rhapsody." As with most of Leroy's compositions, I'll play a composed section, then improvise freely within the context and parameters he gives me. This particular piece alternates chords and harmonies with smooth melodic lines. I want to take you inside the harmonies, so let's divide the audience into three sections. Okay, if you're in this section, your part is this: "Do—Fa—Do—Sol—." Let's try it . . . Good!

Now, if you're in the middle, your part goes like this: "Mi—Fa—Mi—Re—." Sing with me . . . Great!

And if you're on this side, you'll have the soprano line that goes like this: "Sol—La—Sol—Fa—." Everybody!

Great. Now, let's put all three parts together and I'll play the same chords on viola with what's called a *ricochet bowing*. Sustain your notes and watch the scroll of my viola for the changes.

Okay, there's still something missing. If this is jazz, there has to be some improvisation, right? Raise your hand if you play piano. Wow! That's a lot of players. Sir, could you help me out? What I need you to do is sit at the piano, and play some smooth, flowing notes on the white keys. We'll play our chords, pause and let you take a turn, and we'll come back in and keep taking turns. It's impossible for you to make a mistake; just play some smooth and flowing notes. Game? Great; give our volunteer a hand! So, let's make a viola-piano-vocal rhapsody. Here we go. . . .

[**Perform improvisation.**]

DAVID: Wonderful! Give yourselves a hand. So in "Viola Rhapsody," Leroy asks me to play the chords you just learned, then I have to play a double-stop melody that sounds like this [**play a few bars of middle section**], then I'm on my own. He says, "Play chords until you can't play any more chords, then play melody until you can't play any more melody. Just keep alternating." Listen for how much variety can be found just within those two ways of playing. Here's "Viola Rhapsody."

[**Perform "Viola Rhapsody."**]

DAVID: The next work, "Big Wood," was written for solo viola and improvised modern dance. In the school tours, children have actually been improvising dance to my performance, but tonight, we have the privilege of enjoying the improvised choreography of dancers from Saginaw High School. Please give them a warm welcome!

This particular piece uses some of Jenkins' most unusual sound effects, and the dancers have to react accordingly, as they'll demonstrate. Sometimes, I have to make some harsh scratching sounds with the bow; watch how the dancers react. Other times, I'm playing a fast trill while bowing on the bridge to make a raspy sound. Listen for those and many other effects as the dancers and I perform "Big Wood."

[**Perform "Big Wood."**]

DAVID: Thank you. I'm going to conclude the concert with Leroy Jenkins' "Festival Finale," but first I'd like to say a word of thanks to Scott Seeburger of Dow Corning, and Nancy Koepke and Barb Day of the Saginaw Community Enrichment Commission, for making this residency so enjoyable. I'd also like to thank all of you for coming out tonight; you've been an extraordinary audience—especially those of you who are missing the first half of the Red Wings playoff game! Here's Leroy Jenkins' "Festival Finale!"

[**Perform "Festival Finale."**]

APPENDIX A

Interactive Concert Checklist

SCRIPTING AND ACTIVITY DESIGN CHECKLIST:

Does the concert have:

___ a good balance between performance and interaction? (approximately 2/3 music, 1/3 interaction)

___ intentional decisions about theatrical elements? (set, lighting, blocking, etc.)

___ a good program order that creates a nice overall shape?

___ appropriate pacing of musical works and interactions?

___ a culminating piece or activity?

Do we:

___ engage the audience as listeners, co-creators, and co-performers?

___ offer a variety of activity types?

___ offer a variety of activity formats? (whole group, a few volunteers, etc.)

___ address multiple intelligences and modes of perception?

___ include at least one visual aid or visual activity?

___ provide effective transitions from one part to the next?

Do the interactions:

___ provide opportunities for reflection?

___ provide clear entry points and listening foci for every piece?

___ have a significant payoff that makes them worthwhile to the audience?

___ enhance the hearing of the music?

PREPARATION AND LOGISTICS CHECKLIST:

Have we:

___ completely scripted the concert?

___ refined the wording to achieve maximum clarity and conciseness?

___ memorized our script and outline?

___ rehearsed the script and the blocking as seriously as the music?

___ made all performers aware of their roles?

___ tried out the interactions on friends or held an open dress rehearsal?

___ notified our venue's management, stagehands, lighting, or technical crews of any needs?

___ [for school concerts] written and sent a teachers' guide containing information about our group, the concert, the pieces, the composers? Does this guide include simple activities that will enhance our concert?

___ made arrangements to have our concert recorded or videoed?

Assessment and post-concert reflection:

___ Have we made simple assessment forms or surveys for our audiences to fill out so that we get valuable constructive feedback and useful quotes for our press kit?

___ Do we have trustworthy, objective friends to attend and give feedback?

___ Have we set a time to watch the concert video and evaluate it?

APPENDIX B

Annotated Bibliography

Following are some of the sources that have influenced my approach and development as a Teaching Artist and interactive performer. I trust you will find them useful and that you will explore the additional resources that are emerging as our field develops.

Bernstein, Leonard. ***Leonard Bernstein's Young People's Concerts.*** **Edited by Jack Gottlieb. New York: Anchor Books, 1992.**

> This book contains some of Bernstein's greatest scripts and is well worth study. While you're at it, be sure to visit the website www.leonardbernstein.com, where you can purchase video recordings of the *Young People's Concerts* and read his scripts online.

Booth, Eric. ***The Music Teaching Artist's Bible: Becoming a Virtuoso Educator.*** **London: Oxford University Press, 2009.**

> Written by the "Father of Teaching Artistry," Booth's book covers in-depth approaches for musicians seeking to build thriving careers combining high-level artistry with community engagement and educational outreach. Comprehensive in scope, Booth provides wisdom to live by.

Cabaniss, Thomas. "A Teaching Artist Prepares." ***Teaching Artist Journal.*** **1 no. 1 (2003): 31–37.**

> This groundbreaking article is a wonderful and detailed description of the process of brainstorming a work of art and designing activities for engaging listeners and learners.

Pathways to the Orchestra. Thomas Cabaniss and David Wallace, editors. New York: The New York Philharmonic Society, 2002, 2009.

> Written by eleven Teaching Artists in collaboration with five classroom teachers, this three-year curriculum is chock-full of ideas for activities and entry points into musical masterpieces. At the time of this publication, *Pathways to the Orchestra* is available for download at the teacher resources section at www.nyphil.org.

Flagg, Aaron, Thomas Cabaniss, and David Wallace. *New York Philharmonic: An American Celebration: New York Philharmonic Special Edition for Teachers, Vol. 1*. New York: New York Philharmonic Society, 2001.

> President and Executive Director Zarin Mehta writes, "With this *Special Edition for Teachers*, we are proud to make vibrant examples of the American orchestral repertoire available to teachers and students in ways that engage, involve, and inspire." This book and companion CD contain activities and lessons that demonstrate how to build more extensive preparatory workshops around entry points into a particular piece of music. Available at www.nyphil.org.

Flagg, Aaron, Ani Gregorian, Sarah Johnson, and David Wallace. *New York Philharmonic: Bernstein Live!: New York Philharmonic Special Edition for Teachers, Vol. 2*. New York: New York Philharmonic Society, 2002.

> President and Executive Director Zarin Mehta writes, "With this second volume of *Special Edition for Teachers*, we are proud to provide teachers and students with inspired presentations of exceptional live performances by Leonard Bernstein. In his tradition of communicating the joy of music to audiences of all ages, the lessons in this volume will allow you and your students to share in his incomparable musical legacy." Using multiple intelligences and tried-and-true activities, this volume presents additional examples of workshops for exploring musical works. Available at www.nyphil.org.

Gardner, Howard. *Multiple Intelligences: The Theory in Practice.* New York, N.Y.: Basic Books, 1993.

> Every educator should be familiar with Howard Gardner's multiple intelligence theory and its practical application. While there are many authors and topics on the subject, it's always good to go to the primary source.

Green, Barry with W. Timothy Gallwey. *The Inner Game of Music.* Garden City, N.Y.: Doubleday, 1986.

> Barry Green's insightful book contains many strategies for enjoying music as well as conquering stage fright and musical challenges. His clear principles are easily transferable to teaching and interacting with an audience.

Marsalis, Wynton. *Marsalis on Music.* 216 min. Sony Wonder. Videocassette (ASIN 6303640362), 1995. Also on DVD.

> Wynton Marsalis is a charismatic musical ambassador with a heart for teaching. These videos provide us with an exceptional role model who has a natural approach for sharing music with young people.

Robinson, Sarah. *Clubbing for Classical Musicians.* Club Classical Books, Los Angeles, 2014. www.sarahtheflutist.com.

> Sarah Robinson's practical how-to guide for booking yourself in clubs and other venues provides many useful strategies and pointers for engaging audiences in nightclubs and similar venues.

Taylor, Livingston. *Stage Performance.* New York: Pocket Books, 2000.

> Singer, songwriter, and Berklee College of Music professor Livingston Taylor shares his wisdom about serving and captivating an audience. His brother James embodies his advice.

ABOUT THE AUTHOR

Photo by Christopher Davis

Whether playing classical viola with the Chamber Music Society of Lincoln Center, Texas fiddle with the Doc Wallace Trio, electric violin at heavy-metal shows, or contemporary compositions with his flute-viola-harp trio, Hat Trick, David Wallace is at home in front of an audience. Around the globe, musicians have widely adopted his groundbreaking approaches to audience engagement and interactive performance.

David's broadcast credits include NPR, PBS, KTV (Korea), Tokyo MX, WQXR, CBS, and ABC. He has recorded for Arc Music UK, Bridge Records, BIS Records, Innova Recordings, Tzadik Records, Resonance Records, and Mulatta Records. An award-winning composer, David's commissions for original compositions and arrangements include the New York Philharmonic, Carnegie Hall, Suntory Hall, the Marian Anderson String Quartet, and violinist Rachel Barton Pine.

As a teaching artist, David has worked for dozens of arts organizations, including Young Audiences, Lincoln Center Education, and big five orchestras. In 2002, David's numerous creative contributions were honored with the first McGraw-Hill Companies' Robert Sherman Award for Music Education and Community Outreach, honoring musicians who have distinguished themselves as artists and educators.

Currently chair of Berklee College of Music's String Department, Wallace previously enjoyed a fourteen-year tenure as a Juilliard professor, and seventeen years as a New York Philharmonic Teaching Artist.

INDEX

Note: Page numbers in *italics* indicate photos.

A

Adamopoulos, Athena, 37, 38
adults, interactive concerts for, 126–28
   content and, 128
   engaging shy, 127
agenda, fitting a non-musical, 71
Ahmad, Salman, 110–11
American Music Abroad State Department program, 114–15, *117*
Anderson, Marian, 84
anthems, 40
apathy, combating performers', 76
Appel, Andrew, 82–83
arts, future of, 136–37
ASCAP, 84
attention spans, developing, 83
audience engagement
   archetypes and strategies for, 31–50
   asking questions, 19
   concert series, 77, 81–82, 126
   connection increased through interaction, 134
   cultural ambassadorship and exchange, 109–17
   deepening, 77–85
   developing an overall strategy for, 82
   entry point for, 7–11
   experiential, 12–13
   future of the arts and, 136–37
   as mindset, 135–37
   multiple intelligences and, 16–19
   online, 77, 85
   "perform-along" as interactive strategy, 4, 39–40
   pre- and post-concert workshops, 77, 78–80, 83, 132
   precepts for, 89–90
   principles for, 7–22
   projecting your personality, 21
   reflection and, 19–20
   residencies, 77, 82–84
   sample concert transcriptions, 139, 141–54
   short-term vs. long-term community relationships, 77, 82–84
   stage presence and, 53–62
   tapping audience competencies, 14–16, 28
   venues for, 89–108
audience-inappropriate presentations, avoiding, 74–75
audiences
   adult, 126–28
   children (*See* children, performing for)
   in correctional facilities, 96–99
   in hospitals, 92–94
   knowing, 90
   in psychiatric facilities, 94–96
   in religious facilities, 100–2
   respecting, 68–69, 89, 97–99, 100, 102, 103, 124–25, 135
   speaking to, 57–58
authenticity, personal, 91, 103

B

Bach, Johann Sebastian
   cello suites, 43, 96
   Chromatic Fantasy transcribed for viola, 132
   first prelude from *The Well-Tempered Clavier*, 39
   "Largo," 98
   opening movement from harpsichord concerto, 46
   "Prelude in C Major," 142–44
Baez, Joan, 84
Barrett, Sigurd, 48
bars, performing in, 104–5
Bartók, Béla, string quartets, 9–10, 12–13
Bash the Trash, 71
Beethoven, Ludwig van
   Symphony No. 5, 7, 8
   Symphony No. 6, 36
   Symphony No. 9, "Ode to Joy" from, 39
Bellevue Hospital (New York), 95
benefit concerts, 110–11
Bernstein, Leonard, 13, 21, 75, 76, 120, 135
Bertles, John, 71
Bethpage, Long Island, *Conversations with Music* series, 19–20

Biber, Heinrich, *Passacaglia "The Guardian Angel,"* 34, 142, 145–47
bilingual audiences, 113
Bilous, Edward, 21, 64
BMI, 84
bodily/kinesthetic intelligence, 18
Bonanza, Dennis, 98
Bono, 40
Bontrager, Chuck, 48
Bookspan, Janet, 58–59
Boomerang Phrase Sampler, 98
Booth, Eric, 21, 80n, 97n
Boston Pops, 45
Bridgehampton Chamber Music Festival, 37, 38
Brill, Penny, 94
Broken Consort, 100
Brooklyn Academy of Music, 41–42
Brubaker, Bruce, 42
busking, 105–8
   logistics of, 107
   tips for, 108

C

Cabaniss, Thomas, 36
Caesar, Shirley, 47
cafés, performing in, 104–5
call-and-response, 49
Carnegie Hall
   educational programs, 25, 42
   Link-Up programs, 39
Carrick, Richard, 95
Cash, Johnny, 96–97, 99
Center for Arts Education, 9
Chamber Music America, 83, 84
Chapman, Beth Nielsen, "Heads Up for the Wrecking Ball," 98
checklists
   preparation and logistics, 156
   scripting and activity design, 155
Chelsey Green and the Green Project, 115, *117*
Chesis, Linda, 78n
children, performing for
   children's concerts, 20, 40, 41, 60, *60*, 75, 120
   in hospitals, 93
   in schools, 91–92, 110, 124–25
   Young Audiences, 81

Chopin, Fryderyk, *Prelude in E minor, Op. 28*, No. 4, 33
Christopher, Evan, *110*
Chuck D, 84
churches, performing in, 100–102
Classical Jam, 50
Clinton, George, 47
coaching sessions, 40
codes of conduct, respecting, 91, 100
coffee houses, performing in, 104–5
comedy clubs, performing in, 102–4, 126
Community Engagement Lab (CEL), 97–99
composition, interactive, 4
   examples of, 37–39
Concert Artists Guild, 58–59
concert design for interactive performance, 23–30
   activities, 26–29
   brainstorming theme and repertoire, 23–26
   multiple perspectives, 26
   musical relevance and, 28–29
   music-to-interaction ratio, 26
concert series, 77, 81–82, 126
concert transcriptions, 139, 141–54
Cooperstown Chamber Music Festival, 78–79, *79*
Copland, Aaron
   Appalachian Spring, 40, 79
   Fanfare for the Common Man, 4
correctional facilities
   logistics at, 99
   performing in, 96–99
courtesy, 91, 100
Crumb, George, *Black Angels*, 4, 65–66
cultural ambassadorship, 109–17
   importance of, 109
   overcoming language barriers, 112–13
   personal stories, 114–17
cuts, making, 75–76

D

Daugherty, Michael, *UFO*, 59n
Deak, Jon, 60, *60*
demonstration as strategy, 49
demonstration in lieu of discovery, avoiding, 64–66
dialogue-based activities, 46–47
disengaged performers as pitfall, 76
Doc Wallace Trio, 125

E

East, Donna, 102–3
Eighth Blackbird, 47
Eli Yamin Jazz Quartet, *110*
engagement. *See also* audience engagement
  as approach to life, 136–37
  as mindset, 135–37
  entry points for audiences, 7–11
    audience competencies and, 14–16, 28
    for complex or unfamiliar music, 9–10, 13
    designing activities for, 26–29
    examples of, 7–8
    interdisciplinary collaborators and, 44–45
    musical, intellectual/metaphorical, or personal, 31–33
    musical relevance of, 28–29
    potential, 11

F

Fifth House Ensemble, 44
Fisk Jubilee Singers, 24–25
Flobots, 84
Folds, Ben, 39
Fort Wayne Philharmonic, 24
Four Nations Ensemble, *82*, 82–83
Furbee, Erin, 80

G

Gambill, Paul, 97n
games as interactive strategy, 49–50
Gardner, Howard, *Frames of Mind*, 17–18
Gershwin, George, "Summertime," 142, 152–53
Gil Evans Orchestra, 41
Glennie, Evelyn, 59n
Gounod, Charles, "Ave Maria," 39
gratitude, 90
Green, Chelsey, 115–16, *117*
Griffin, Stephanie, 92
Grissom, Sean, 106–7, 108

H

Haggard, Merle, 96–97
Handel, George Frideric, *Messiah*, 39
Hansen, Nikolaj, 48
Heidelberg Catechism, 101
Hendrix, Jimi, 41–42
Hines, Justin, 112–13
Hodsden, James, 101
Hong-Park, Jihea, 112
hospitals, performing in, 92–94
Hudson Valley Philharmonic, 35, 42, 71
  children's concerts, 40, 41

I

Ice Cube, "It Was a Good Day," 40
improvisation, interactive, 4
  examples of, 36–37
  in psychiatric facilities, 96
  sample concert transcription, 141–54
Improvisational Journey interaction concert, 141–54
intelligences, multiple, 16–19
interactive performance
  for adults, 126–28
  archetypes and strategies, 31–50
  audience connection and, 134
  audience engagement principles, 7–22
  common questions about, 119–24
  concert transcriptions, 139, 141–54
  dealing with reluctant group members, 121–24
  deepening audience engagement, 77–85
  defined, 3–6
  designing, 23–30
  developing an engaging stage presence, 53–62
  distinguished from lecture-demonstration, 3, 5
  examples of successful, 4
  finding time to prepare, 128–29
  gaining skill, 119–21
  getting bookings for, 130–31
  getting started, 119
  music as communication, 137
  musical relevance in, 28–29, 42–43, 69–71
  pedagogical uses for, 131–32
  philosophical opposition to, 123–24
  post-performance assessment, 30
  practicing, 120
  preparation and logistics checklist, 156
  scripting and activity design checklist, 155
  scripting and rehearsing, 29–30
  selectivity in, 129–30, 133–34
  theatrical elements, 55, 56
  venues for, 89–108
  videos of, 120

interdisciplinary approaches as interactive strategy, 43–45
interpersonal intelligence, 18
interpreter, working with an, 113
intrapersonal intelligence, 18
irrelevant activities, avoiding, 71–72

J

James, Jerry, 9
jargon, avoiding, 64, 74–75
Jazz at Lincoln Center, 114
Jazz Power Initiative, 114
Jenkins, Leroy, works by, 142, 153–54

K

Kapilow, Robert, 128
Kodály, Zoltán, viola transcription of Bach's *Chromatic Fantasy*, 132

L

Lamb's Theatre (New York), 103
language barriers, overcoming, 112–13
Law, Wendy, 50
League of American Orchestras, 84
lecture series, 128
lecture-demonstration, interactive performance distinguished from, 3, 5
León, Tania, 36
lessons, interactive strategies for private, 131–32
Levy, Daniel, 125
light shows, 42
Lila Wallace Foundation, 136
listening challenges and activities as interactive strategy, 35
logical/mathematical intelligence, 17–18

M

Ma, Yo-Yo, 43, *44*
Manhattan School of Music, 25, 49, 50, 67
Marsalis, Wynton, 120
McClurkin, Donny, 47
McFerrin, Bobby, 39, 72
McKay, Glenn, 42
Medeski, Martin, and Wood, 41
Mendelssohn, Felix
    The Hebrides overture, 41
    Italian Symphony, 72
"*Messiah* sings," 39
metaphors as entry points, 11
Millán, Luis, 141–54
Montclair State University, *54*

Moon, Beata, *32*
Muir String Quartet, 45
multimedia as interactive strategy, 41–43
    finding collaborators, 45
    musical relevance in, 42–43
    pitfalls of, 43
Music and Wellness program, Pittsburgh, 94
music therapy, 94
Music Unlocked! collective, 104
musical elements as entry points, 11
musical quotations, 4
musical/rhythmic intelligence, 18
musician audition as interactive strategy, 40–41
musician coaching as interactive strategy, 40
MWROC, 48

N

National Arts Centre (Ottawa), 113
National Endowment for the Arts, 83
New World Symphony, 126
New York Philharmonic, 59n
    Learning Overtures residency, 112
    "Ode to Joy" sing-alongs, 39
    School Day concerts, *6*, 72
    A Silk Road to China interactive concert, *44*
    Special Editions for Teachers, 132
    Teaching Artist Ensemble, 25, 49
    Young People's Concerts, 20, 40, 60, *60*, 75, 120
Newband, *54*, 54–55
Nietzsche, Friedrich, *Also sprach Zarathustra*, 29
nightclubs, performing in, 104–5, 126
Niigata University (Japan), 112–13
92nd Street Y (New York), 104
non-musical focus, avoiding or mitigating, 69–71

O

"On Top of Old Smokey," 96
online engagement, 77, 85
orchestral musicians, finding, 129
Oregon Symphony, 80
outreach concerts
    international, *110*, 110–12
    "one-shot," 77
    respecting, 68–69

P

Pachelbel, Johann, *Canon in D*, 35
Paganini, Niccolò
   24 Caprices for Solo Violin, 133–34
   "Caprice No. 24," 142, 149–50
paired pieces as interactive strategy, 45
Parliament-Funkadelic, 47
Partch, Harry, 54–55
partnerships, building, 91
"perform-alongs," 4, 39–40
performance venues, 89–108
   bars, cafés, coffee houses, nightclubs, 104–5, 126
   bilingual, 113
   busking, 105–8
   comedy clubs, 102–4, 126
   correctional facilities, 96–99
   familiarizing with, 90
   hospitals, 92–94
   psychiatric facilities, 94–96
   religious facilities and communities, 100–102
   schools, 91–92, 110, 124–25
Perlman, Itzhak, 21
Perry, Chris, 80
personality, projecting your, 21
Piaggio, Carina, 71
piece lengths, problematic, 75–76
piece simulation as interactive strategy, 34
Pine, Rachel Barton, 133–34
   "Introduction, Theme, and Variations on *God Defend New Zealand*," 133
"ping-ponging," 58
pitfalls, avoiding, 63–76
   audience-inappropriate presentation, 74–75
   demonstration in lieu of discovery, 64–66
   disengaged performers, 76
   irrelevant activities, 71–72
   lack of variety, 73–74
   non-musical focus, 69–71
   problematic piece lengths, 75–76
   too many words, 63–64
   under-rehearsed lines, 66–67
   under-rehearsed music, 67–69
Pittsburgh Symphony, 94
Plato, 94
post-performance assessment, 30
Prestini, Paola, 44
problems as interactive strategy, 50
program order, adjusting, 29
psychiatric facilities, performing in, 94–96
puzzles as interactive strategy, 50

R

reflection, using time for, 19–20
rehearsing a concert, 30
Reid, Vernon, 41
relationships, building, 91, 102
religious facilities and communities, 100–102
remote control game, 50
repeating pieces as interactive strategy, 45–46
repertoire, concert
   brainstorming, 23–26
   finalizing, 25–26
requests, taking, 46
residencies
   international, 112–13
   long-term, 77, 83–84, 104
   short-term, 82–83
Rhythm Road, The: American Music Abroad, 114–15
Rimsky-Korsakov, Nikolai, *Flight of the Bumblebee*, 41
Ritscher, Karen, 61
Robinson, Sarah, *Clubbing for Classical Musicians*, 105
Rossini, Gioacchino, *William Tell Overture*, 40
Roth, David Lee, 47–48

S

Saginaw Bay Youth Orchestra Chamber Group, 141–54
Saint-Saëns, Camille, *Carnival of the Animals*, 40, 49
Samba vs. Tango event, 80
San Quentin State Prison, 96–97
Schelling, Ernest, 20
schools, performing in, 91–92, 110
   misbehavior and, 124–25
   pedagogical uses for interactive strategies, 131–32
Schulhoff, Erwin, *Concertino for Flute, Viola, and Double Bass*, 50
Scofidio, Dana, 90
Scott-Melnyk, Stephanie, 136n

scripting a concert, 29–30
    concision in, 63–64
    for foreign audiences, 112–13
    reluctant or disruptive group members and, 122–23
    sample transcriptions, 139, 141–54
Seeger, Pete, 13, 39, 84
Shaham, Gil, 69
sharing, 89–90
Sherwood, Kay, 136n
silence, using, 58
Silverman, Tracy, 97–99
sing-alongs, 39, 93
Smetana, Bedrich, *Vltava (The Moldau)*, 42–43
space, performance, 53–54
speaking, effective, 57–58
    in interviews, 78
    practicing, 121
Springsteen, Bruce, 46
St. Victor, Sandra, 41
stage presence, developing an engaging, 53–62
    effective movement, 58–62
    effective speaking, 57–58
    performance space and, 53–54
    practice and, 61, 120–21
State Department, U.S., *110*, 114–16
Stomp, 45
Strauss, Richard, *Also sprach Zarathustra*, 28–29, 33
Stravinsky, Igor
    Petrouchka, 49
    The Rite of Spring, 45
Strom, Yale, 100
"Sweet Georgia Brown," 4
synagogues, performing in, 100

T

Tanglewood Music Festival, 4, 36
    Family Concerts, 41
Tchaikovsky, Pyotr, *Romeo and Juliet Fantasy Overture*, 35
Telemann, Georg Philipp, *Viola Concerto in G Major*, 142, 148
Texas-style contest fiddling, 142, 150–52

theme, concert, 23–26
    criteria for, 23
    examples of, 24–25
Tilson Thomas, Michael, *14*
Toastmasters, 121
Tuttle, Karen, 132

U

U2, "40," 40
under-rehearsed lines, avoiding, 66–67
under-rehearsed music, avoiding, 67–69
underscoring as interactive strategy, 47–48
United Nations, concerts at, 110–11

V

Van Halen, "Ice Cream Man," 47–48
variety, avoiding lack of, 73–74
verbal/linguistic intelligence, 17
verbosity, avoiding, 63–64
VisionIntoArt company, 44
visual activities/visual aids as interactive strategy, 41
Visual Thinking Strategies (VIS), 19n
visual/spatial intelligence, 17
voiceover as interactive strategy, 47–48
Voxare Quartet, 50

W

Walker, Chris, 136n
Wallace, David, 6, 141–54
    Black-Key Improvisation, 142, 144–45
    Nahum: An Apocalyptic Prophesy for Electric Violin or Viola, 48
Wallgriff Duo, 92
Washington Post article on busking, 105–6
Webern, Anton, *Six Bagatelles*, 45
Weingarten, Gene, 105n
Williams, Hank, "Your Cheatin' Heart," 8
Wood, Mark, 48
workshops, pre- and post-concert, 77, 78–80, 83, 132
    ideas for, 80
Wu Man, 44

Y

Yamin, Eli, 24, 114–15
Ying Quartet, 83
Young Audiences, 81